AUSTIN
The Counties Years

by Stewart J. Brown and David Whyley

Published by

Arthur Southern Ltd. • The Austin Counties Car Club

SVANEFJELL

Contents

Introduction 4

Austin - the background 5

The first postwar cars 6

The Austin trucks 10

1947: the first Counties cars 11

The big cars 18

Pedal cars 19

1948: The Hampshire arrives 20

Launch of a dollar earner 23

Taxi! 25

Truck progress 26

Showrooms, parts and servicing 27

1950: Hereford ousts Hampshire 28

A40 Sports 30

1951: a new Seven is launched 32

New assembly building 34

1952: the last real Austin 36

The end of an era 42

BMC 43

New-look A125 43

The end 44

more and more, people are saying...

AUSTIN
– you can depend on it!

THE AUSTIN MOTOR CO LTD • LONGBRIDGE • BIRMINGHAM

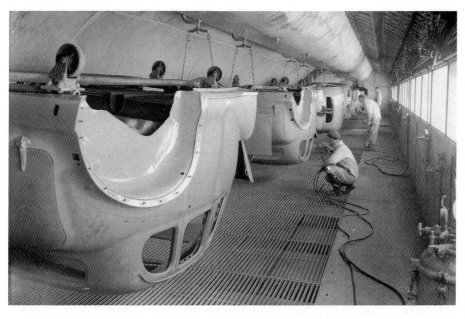

Front Cover: The new A40 Somerset at Tanworth in Arden in 1952.

Back cover (upper, right): The A40 Devon was a best-seller for Austin at home and abroad.

Back cover (upper, left): The A90 Atlantic was aimed at the US market. An early left-hand-drive example with single-piece windscreen poses with a very un-American background.

Back cover (lower): The attractive A40 Somerset coupé, bodied by Carbodies, was a full four-seater.

A new paint plant was installed for the Devon and Dorset bodies. Costing £120,000, it allowed Austin to switch from cellulose to synthetic paint. The bodies travelled through the paint bay suspended from an overhead conveyer travelling at 7 ft per minute. Rotating cradles gave the painters good access to the whole body. With double–shifting, the plant could handle 1,600 bodies per week - in its first 9 months it was used to paint 30,000 bodies.

First published 1992
ISBN 0 - 946265 - 18-6
© Stewart J. Brown and David Whyley, 1992
Typeset in Times and Helvetica
Electronic page makeup by Jeremy Scott
Printed by Metro Press, Edinburgh

Published by
Arthur Southern Ltd. and the Austin Counties Car Club
Distributed by
Arthur Southern Ltd.
5 Hallcroft Close, Ratho, Newbridge
Midlothian EH28 8SD

Introduction

AUSTIN'S EARLY POSTWAR cars have an enduring popularity. They were inexpensive to buy and to run. They were durable and dependable. They epitomise a bygone era in British motoring and in British motor manufacturing.

This book is published to mark the 40th anniversary of two significant events. In 1952 Austin launched the last of its popular series of cars named after English counties. The A40 Somerset was unveiled in February 1952 and replaced the 4 year old Devon. It was arguably the last real Austin, because the other significant event of 1952 was the merger of Austin with the Nuffield Group, makers of Morris, MG, Riley and Wolseley, to form the British Motor Corporation. BMC is the progenitor of the 1990s Rover Group.

The bulk of the photographic material in this book is from the archives of the Rover Group, whose John Chasemore was exceedingly helpful, and from the collections of the compilers, aided by other willing individuals whose contributions are listed below. Austin's chief photographer in the late 1940s and early 1950s was Ron Beach and tribute has to be paid to his skill. Not only did he photograph Austin's cars, often working against impossibly tight deadlines, but he was an accomplished landscape photographer, as early 1950s copies of *The Austin Magazine* bear witness.

Most of the people who helped in the preparation of this book are active members of the Austin Counties Car Club, whose aim is to encourage the restoration and continued use of Austins of the 1939-54 period, and we would particularly like to mention Simon Angel, Tony Collings, Vernon Cox, Denis Cremer, Ray Dawes, Stan Fincham, Steve Frearson, Peter Grimsdale, Ian Hamilton, Norman Milne, Royston Morgan, Peter Ridgway, Andrew Sheppard, David Stoves, Chris Tallents, Brian Swann, Dennis Vowles of the J40 Car Club and, from Australia, Allan Waller. All willingly made material available or provided information which has been included in this album. Don Arrand of the Northfield Society provided information on Austin's housing.

Hazel Gore of British Motor Industry Heritage Trust, an avowed Austin enthusiast, was also particularly helpful and unlocked a few doors for us. Most of the photographs are copyright © Rover Group and are reproduced with the kind permission of BMIHT. Help was also given by archivist Anders Clausager. Former Austin employees willingly talked to us about the Counties period - Doug Adams, Roger Lewis (with his son David) and George Coates, a skilled motor mechanic who spent 50 years with the company and was actively involved in many of Austin's postwar publicity stunts including the Atlantic's Indianapolis run, the Devon at Montlhery and the round-the-world Sports and who more than 20 years after retiring recalls Austin's great days with undisguised delight.

This book deals with the distant days when Britain's currency was measured in pounds, shillings and pence and for ease of reading we have decided not to have modern decimal equivalents intruding in the text. For those who never knew or can't remember the old coinage there were 12 pennies to a shilling and 20 shillings to a pound. A guinea was 21s. One old penny (1d) is equal to 2.4p; one shilling (1s) to 5p. The page headings are based on the style used by Austin for its service journals of the period.

Just over 1,000,000 cars of the Counties range and its predecessors were built by Austin. Fewer than 2,000 survive. The choice of material is designed to create something of the ethos of the period. We hope you enjoy reading it as much as we enjoyed putting it together.

Stewart J. Brown, Framilode, Gloucestershire
David Whyley, Stourbridge, Worcestershire

Ron Beach, the man in charge of Austin's photographic department.

Authors Stewart Brown *(left)* and David Whyley *(right)* with their cars.

Austin - the background

HERBERT AUSTIN (1866-1941) was born in Great Missenden, Buckinghamshire. After working in Australia for the Wolseley Sheep Shearing Machine Co., he returned to Britain and became the company's manager in 1893. In the mid-1890s he produced the Wolseley tri-car (a copy of a French Leon Bollée design). Other cars followed until he left the Wolseley company in 1905 at the age of 39, setting up his own car production in a factory in Longbridge, to the south of Birmingham.

This expanded, with production reaching 576 cars a year in 1910. The company grew dramatically during World War I and in a bold move to ease conditions at a time when there were no skilled tradesmen available to build new houses, Austin bought 200 Readi-Cut wooden prefabricated houses from the Aladdin company in Michigan which were assembled in Northfield. Birmingham City Council gave temporary permission for their erection in 1917; they still stand 75 years later.

Despite a setback after World War I - which saw the company in the hands of receivers - Austin continued to grow. Prewar production had peaked at 963 cars in 1912/13; by 1925/26 output was approaching 25,000 cars, thanks to the legendary Seven which first appeared in 1922. Austin production crossed the 50,000 mark in 1932/33 and reached an inter-war peak of 90,000 in 1936/37.

General Motors, before buying Vauxhall, made a bid for Austin - which was rejected. Sir Herbert Austin became Lord Austin of Longbridge in 1936 and in 1938 - by which time he was 72 - recruited 42 year-old Leonard Lord, who had headed the rival Morris business, as works director. Lord rose rapidly - joint managing director in 1942, deputy chairman in 1943 and chairman in 1945. Under Lord's leadership the Austin board sanctioned a massive £1 million investment for modernization of the company and its products in April 1945. It was Lord who masterminded the merger of Austin and the Nuffield Group and who quickly took over the chairmanship of the new British Motor Corporation.

BMC slowly rationalised the ranges which it had inherited, but pursued a policy which saw marque names and the associated dealer networks preserved. Historians often deal unkindly with BMC's policy of badge engineering, but with strong brand loyalty and minimal foreign competition it doubtless seemed like a good move at the time.

The Austin name was, indeed, the last of the BMC marques to disappear, surviving for almost 40 years after the company was merged with Nuffield to form BMC in 1952.

Austin's stand at the 1948 Motor Show in London's Earls Court. In the centre is the new Atlantic with two of the new Hampshires (top and bottom left), a Sheerline, and two Devons. An A40 chassis stands in the foreground.

The first postwar cars

AS WITH MOST British car makers, Austin's first postwar cars were effectively re-introductions of prewar models. In Austin's case this meant the new range which had been launched in the spring and summer of 1939 with a strong family resemblance across the models. Smallest was the Eight, available with two doors at £128, four doors at £139 or as an open tourer at £132 10s. This replaced the most famous Austin of all time, the Seven, and used an uprated version of the 1937 Big Seven side-valve engine, increased in capacity from 747cc to 900cc and producing 24bhp at 4,400rpm. Production of the Eight started in February 1939 and was followed in May by the 1125cc 32bhp Ten and then in August by the bigger 1535cc 40bhp Twelve. The Ten and Twelve were four-door saloons, although there was also a short-lived Ten tourer. The Eight and Ten had a boxed-in platform type chassis which was integrated with the body structure; the Twelve had a more conven-

tional chassis frame. All had leaf springs and rigid axles front and rear.

Production had barely got under way when it was halted by the outbreak of war - at least as far as the Twelve was concerned. The Eight and Ten found a continued lease of life as military vehicles and were supplied to the War Department for use by the armed forces. Many of these were open tourers. When Eight production came to a halt in 1942 the company had built just over 47,500.

The 1939 models were certainly a styling advance on their predecessors but they still featured separate running boards, a feature abandoned by some other builders, and all had side valve engines. They also were the first Austins to feature what were commonly known as alligator bonnets, in which the bonnet top was hinged at the rear and lifted up from the front.

Much of Longbridge's capacity was turned over to supporting Britain's war effort. It produced

Its appeal is obviously in direct ratio to the comfortable and practical accommodation afforded for four people and the economical running that an engine of this size gives. It is thoroughly equipped, well finished and, a far from inconsiderable point, has behind it the name gained by Austin's for producing a sound type of car.

- from The Autocar road test of the Eight, 24 February 1939.

The Ten finishing line in 1945 in what was known as the Trentham factory. The first cars for civilian consumption receive final attention with K-series military trucks in the background. A painter is touching up the matt khaki paint of the ambulance.

A 1945 view of the postwar Eight, offered only as a four-door saloon.

The Eight and Ten had a platform type chassis which was integrated with the bodywork. This is an Eight.

Although production was being hampered by material shortages, in November 1946 Austin was able to point to increasing output and marked a new high with the completion of 20,000 cars in only 10 weeks.

The Twelve looked like an enlarged Ten, which is effectively what it was with a longer wheelbase and bigger body. The glass louvres at the top of the doors were designed to cut draughts when driving with the window ajar.

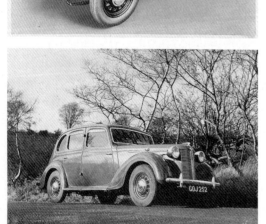

The Twelve and Sixteen offered armchair comfort - almost literally. The arms could be raised to ease access, or to squeeze in a third front seat passenger.

ammunition and ammunition boxes as well as components for such diverse items of military equipment as mines and tanks. A shadow factory at nearby Cofton Hackett built planes. Austin was responsible for the production of 2,866 aircraft comprising:

Fairey Battle fighter/bomber	1229
Stirling bomber	720
Lancaster bomber	330
Hurricane fighter	587

Production of the Eight (four-door only), Ten and Twelve restarted in August 1945, along with another similar car, the Sixteen, which used the Twelve body shell. While the smaller models betrayed Austin's basic conservatism with side valve engines which were improved versions of those used in their predecessors, the Sixteen had a new four-cylinder 2199cc overhead-valve engine, the first to be used in an Austin car and a development from a 1939 six-cylinder engine designed for the company's new truck range and planned for installation in its four-cylinder guise in a wartime Jeep-type vehicle. It was initially rated at 58bhp but this was raised to 67bhp from April 1946. The Sixteen had an integral hydraulic jacking system.

In February 1946 the cars were being advertised at £323 for the Eight, £397 for the Ten, £531 for the Twelve, and £569 for the Sixteen. All were four-dour models with what were quaintly described as sliding heads - which would be known to a later generation as sunroofs. Exports were crucial to the war-ravaged British economy and were to play a pivotal role in Austin's success in the late 1940s and early 1950s. At this early stage Austin was already claiming to have built around two-thirds of all the British cars which had been exported since the war ended: in the seven months from June 1945 Austin contributed 2,124 cars to the UK motor industry's export total of 3,150.

Production was being carried out against a background of material shortages. Pleas for more steel were to become a common motor industry cry, and at Austin the Longbridge works were shut down for part of February 1947 because of a lack

The Sixteen used the same body as the Twelve but with a new overhead valve engine, the first in an Austin car. It was the last Austin to have rear-hinged front doors. This is alongside the thatched boat house at Rednal in August 1945.

The Longbridge showroom in 1945 with the postwar range, including two K-series trucks, on display. In the centre of the floor is a Sixteen chassis with two industrial engines, an 8hp and a 10hp, in the foreground.

of coal.

The Austin Eight was an economical little car. A test by *The Light Car* magazine in October 1947 carried the headline "50mpg with an Austin Eight". There was a catch: the 50mpg figure was obtained at a constant 20mph. But overall the Eight returned a creditable average of 39.9mpg on a 359 mile run. Best cruising speed was described as 40-45mph. By this time the price was £358 10s 6d. This of course has to be seen against a background of petrol at 2s a gallon (and still rationed) at a time when there were only 1,858,000 cars on Britain's roads - a number which would increase ten-fold in the following 40 years.

The Eight and Ten were also produced as vans, with capacities of 6cwt and 10cwt respectively. The Ten van used a bored-out version of the saloon engine which increased its size from 1125cc to 1237cc. All four models could be provided as chassis-scuttles for the provision of coach-built wooden-framed estate cars. A factory-built Sixteen estate car - which introduced the Countryman name to the Austin range - was also available, but few were built.

One side effect of the emphasis on exports was that demand for new cars in Britain far exceeded supply, resulting in lengthy waiting lists. To curb profiteering by people who acquired new cars and immediately resold them at inflated prices, the British Motor Trade Association introduced a covenant in 1946 which prevented a new car from being resold until it was 12 months old. However even 12 month old cars attracted a premium on the used car market. Sixteens, costing £569 new in 1947, were typically being advertised at prices from £935 to £1,175 in 1948.

Production of the Sixteen lasted until 1949, but the three smaller models were dropped in 1947, to make way for the brand new A40 Devon. The Eight was the last Austin to use six volt electrics. Austin's 1,000,000th car was a Sixteen, produced in 1946. It was painted with a matt cream finish, signed by most of the company's employees and kept as a museum piece.

Driving became a positive nightmare; the gale increased in fury; the snow froze on our headlamps; for a while we had to have the screen open in order to see anything at all; and the road turned into a slanting uneven sheet of ice. The gaps between the snow-drifts on either side seemed to get even narrower, and really one drives more by guess-work than anything else. By now it was pitch dark and the heavy snow was blown at us with such force that when our headlamps illuminated anything at all, which was only when the caked snow on their glass became so heavy that on going over a bump in the ice it got knocked off, it seemed as though we were penetrating into the heart of some fantastic firework.
- *Alan Hess, writing in Gullible's Travels.*

The 1,000,000th Austin - a matt cream Sixteen which was signed by Longbridge employees - flanked by the 999,999th, a Ten, and the 1,000,001st. Note the appropriate registration numbers. The photograph is dated 25 July 1946.

The driving position of the Eight. The handle in the centre of the dashboard is for opening the windscreen - a feature soon to disappear from saloon cars - and the circular hook above the centre door pillar raises the rear window blind. The main dial in front of the driver is the speedometer (calibrated to 70mph); the three displays on the left hand dial are marked oil, amperes and petrol. The metal dashboard has a mock wood grain finish.

The Sixteen starred in the first of a number of high-profile publicity escapades organised by Austin's energetic public relations officer, Alan Hess. In 1947 he planned a 3,000 mile seven capitals in seven days European tour, using three Sixteens which ran from Oslo via Stockholm, Copenhagen, Amsterdam, Brussels and Paris to Geneva, finishing at the Geneva Motor Show. The roads were still in very poor condition because of war damage - and even the weather was against the cars, with unusually severe blizzards for March. But they made it.

In his account of the journey, *Gullible's Travels*, Alan Hess describes what was clearly a gruelling experience including 33 hours of continuous driving at an average speed of 13mph in Germany where there were snowdrifts, ice, an 80mph gale and floods to contend with.

The Eight was Austin's best-seller in the early postwar years, with over 56,000 being built in just three years. The Ten was close behind at 55,500, while the larger Twelve managed just over 8,500. Sixteen production totalled almost 35,500.

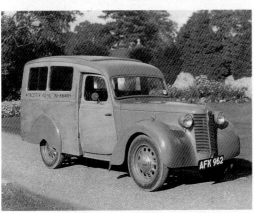

A freezing cold day in March 1947, and three Sixteens fitted with radiator muffs stand on the quayside at Newcastle-on-Tyne, waiting to be loaded on the Jupiter in readiness for the run to seven European capitals in seven days. Alan Hess, who masterminded the run, is second from the right.

Left, from top:
The Ten was available as a chassis for specialist bodywork. Its versatility is illustrated by a milk float for Curborough Dairy in Staffordshire, an estate car for Worcester Royal Infirmary and a wooden-bodied shooting brake. All were built in 1946. Note the absence of a bumper and polished trim on the bonnet sides and radiator of the two commercial vehicles. They also have painted rather than chromed headlamps.

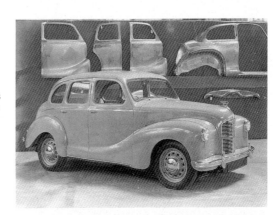

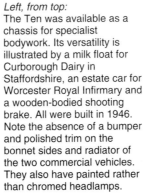

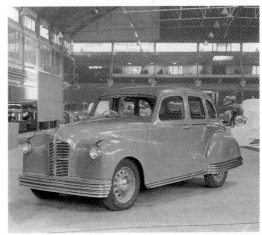

Right, from top:
As part of Austin's quest for a Sixteen replacement a number of prototypes were developed in the autumn of 1947. Devon panels were used on this vehicle and, with some considerable modification on another which had a heavy trans-Atlantic influence with brightwork around the skirt. A third was a sleek two-door car which bore strong hints of the style to be unveiled on the new A70 Hampshire whose launch was only 12 months away. They were photographed in the service workshop at Longbridge.

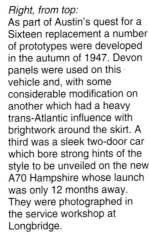

The Austin trucks

NOT ONLY WERE Austin's prewar cars revived after the war; so too were its trucks. These had been launched in 1939 and had featured a new 3459cc six-cylinder overhead valve engine rated at 67.5bhp. The smaller of the two was the 2-3 ton capacity K2; the larger the 5-ton K4. A coach chassis was also offered. All were of normal control layout and bore more than a passing resemblance to the popular Bedford O-series trucks - which was hardly surprising since Austin had recruited Bedford's designer.

Truck production continued throughout the war years, totalling around 75,000 vehicles, including a number of models which had been developed specifically for military use. But after the war it was the 11ft 2in wheelbase K2 and 13ft 1.25in wheelbase K4 which re-appeared on the civilian market. A 5-ton tipper variant was available with an intermediate wheelbase of 9ft 3in. The K-series trucks had Lockheed hydraulic brakes, with servo assistance on the 5-ton K4. The engine was bored out to 3993cc during the war and this, as used on the A125 and producing 68bhp, became standard

on K-series chassis from 1948. The 5-ton model was also offered with a 4.73-litre 70bhp Perkins P6 diesel engine.

Production of the 2-ton K2 averaged 7,700 annually during its best years, 1946-50, falling to around 4,500 in the early 1950s. The 5-ton K4 did rather better, reaching a peak of almost 15,000 in the 1950-51 production year and averaging over 10,000 a year. The coach variant of the K4 was the 15ft wheelbase CXB but a few K4s were bodied as coaches and some were modified by coachbuilders to forward-control layout.

The K range was expanded in 1946 to include the forward-control K8 25cwt van powered by the 2199cc Sixteen engine rated at 65bhp. Girling hydraulic brakes were fitted. The 300cu ft steel body had doors on both sides and on the rear, giving rise to the name Three-Way van. The K8 was also offered as a chassis with or without a cab and a number were bodied as ambulances and 16-seat coaches. A total of 27,000 K8s were built during the model's seven year production run. Output was at it highest between 1948 and 1951.

The K-series trucks had a strong resemblance to Bedford's popular O-series range and were powered by a six-cylinder ohv petrol engine. This is a 1946 5-tonner with drop-side bodywork.

Right: A minority of K4 chassis were fitted with coach bodywork, to rival Bedford's OB coach model. Jones Brothers of Wednesfield, who traded as Happy Times Coaches, ran this example with bodywork by Plaxton of Scarborough. It was a 29-seater and weighed only 3 tons 17cwt unladen.

Far right: The prototype of the K8 25cwt van in August 1946 was close to the finalised design. The main differences are in the grille, which only had vertical bars in the centre section on production models; the doors which had recessed handles; and the step below the door.

Right: A production K8 van for drinks deliveries in Gibraltar. A number of K8s were bodied as passenger vehicles.

Far Right: This ambulance was delivered to Worcestershire County Council in 1949. Only the driver gets a windscreen wiper.

1947: the first Counties cars

THE AUSTIN A40 Devon and Dorset were the first totally new family cars to be launched in postwar Britain. They appeared in the autumn of 1947. At a time when petrol was still rationed and most cars were black, the launch material included a brochure called *Colour comes back to motoring*. It waxed lyrical:

"Finished in a thermo-plastic flow-gloss enamel of high lustre, more weatherproof and sparkling than buffed cellulose, each model is available in a choice of five colours, while the seating, carpets, instruments and controls are all *en suite*, to give an air of modern elegance, not hitherto achieved in a car of this class."

The colours on offer were burgundy, Portland grey, Royal blue, Mist green and, of course, black. Some years were to pass before black disappeared from the colour ranges on popular cars and then still later reappeared as an extra-cost option.

However the real advances on the new A40 were more than a range of pretty colours. The four-door Devon and two-door Dorset were new from end to end - chassis, engine and body. The Devon had what was still known as a six-light body (with three windows on either side). But the new A40s brought Austin's styling totally up-to-date. Gone were the separate wings, headlights and running boards of the prewar models; in their place was a smoothly-styled body with flowing lines. The achievement of this new look was described in a contemporary brochure:

"With Austin cars this calls for handsome yet honest design, avoiding airy flamboyance on the one hand or sombre dignity on the other."

Some of the larger pressings for the new bodies as well as some of the sub-assemblies were produced by Pressed Steel at Cowley and by Fisher & Ludlow of Castle Bromwich.

The engine was new, a 1200cc overhead-valve unit which quickly earned an enviable reputation for durability, albeit with a tendency to blow the occasional cylinder head gasket. The engine's power output, 40bhp at 4,300rpm, was the source of the A40 model designation, although early prototypes were in fact badged as Tens, using the traditional RAC hp rating which was based on a theoretical formula worked around the engine's bore size. The A40 effectively combined the power of the Twelve with the economy of the Ten, both of which it replaced, along with the smaller Eight. The new ohv engine gave the A40 a power output of 33.3bhp per litre, compared with 28.4bhp per litre for the old side-valve Ten - an increase of 17 per cent - and with the added benefit of power over a much wider range of engine speeds thanks to the overhead valve layout.

The chassis had independent front suspension, an innovation for Austin. It also had a conventional frame, unlike the integrated floor pan of the Eight and Ten, which could in some ways be seen as a retrograde step. Girling hydro-mechanical brakes were fitted. The Devon was launched at £441 11s 8d - plus £7 13s 4d if you wanted the luxury of a heater. This at a time when annual road tax for cars first registered after 1 January 1947 had just been fixed at a flat rate of £10 from 1 January 1948 irrespective of engine size, replacing the previous graduated rates. Every silver lining has a cloud and with the flat rate road tax came a punitive double purchase tax on new cars costing over £1,000.

Although the Devon and the Dorset shared the same chassis and running gear, the Dorset was launched with a 4in narrower track than the Devon and the prototypes had narrower bodywork too. This was not quite as strange as it sounded; despite the strong similarity in their styling, the two models shared few common body panels. However when production actually got under way, the Dorset's width was increased to match that of the Devon.

At the dealer launch of the new cars the width difference was still planned for production. Leonard Lord said: "Whilst very different outwardly, in fundamentals these two new cars are identical in design. True, the Devon has four doors whilst the Dorset has two, but both models are of the same wheelbase and have the same type of frame and rear axle, the only difference being that the Dorset is four inches narrower in track than the Devon. Both models have exactly the same engine and transmission. The 12 volt electrical systems are identical and the tooling is very much the same for both bodies."

Lord continued: "The benefit of this standardisation is naturally reflected in their price and quality, and the speed of our changeover from the old to the new production. It will be obvious from this policy your servicing problems will be greatly simplified and stocks of parts will become more compact."

The new models were an instant success. In April 1948 *The Light Car* carried out a road test on a Devon which led its tester to comment: "With this A40 model the Austin concern has set a new standard by which future cars in the small family

Compared with the old models, these new ones have interior heating and ventilation, independent front suspension, concealed door hinges and running boards, interior locking control of the bonnet, and many other refinements. We obviously don't believe that because the car is small it need of necessity be austere.
- Leonard Lord, launching the A40 Devon and Dorset

November 1946, and the new A40 takes shape - although still described as an Eight. The production Dorset, launched 12 months later, differed little from this wooden mock-up.

I still think the market in this country is largely for small cars, in spite of all that has been said to the contrary.
- Leonard Lord, October 1947

saloon class will be judged". Similarly *The Motor* said that "its performance may be regarded as setting a postwar standard for competitively priced cars in this class". Praise indeed. Fuel consumption was 32mpg.

The only real problem related to the independent front suspension, the design of which was causing excessive tyre wear. Track tests, including punishing pavé runs in Belgium, soon had the problem solved.

Initially the bulk of Austin's output went abroad - notably to North America and Australia - as Britain's postwar government continued to put the emphasis on exports. In February 1948 the government announced that steel would only be allocated to car manufacturers who were exporting 75 per cent of their production; the figure had previously been 50 per cent. Of the first 30,000 A40s built only 1,000 were for the home market.

In February 1948 Austin claimed that its export earnings amounted to £115 per minute which on the current food rationing system meant that the effort of each Austin employee was enough to feed 187 of his fellow countrymen for a week. Rationing, introduced in 1940, started to ease in 1948 (bread and jam were de-rationed) but didn't end until 1954. Austin's March claim was that in

that month it had exported 5,722 vehicles worth more than £2 million, a record for any British motor manufacturer. This record was quickly broken - the May figure was 6,071 vehicles valued at £2.25 million. The 100,000th postwar export Austin arrived in the USA in June, bringing the company's postwar export earnings to over £30 million. The broad breakdown of exports was:

Europe	30,000
The Americas	23,000
Asia	18,000
Australasia	16,000
Africa	13,000

The 20,000th postwar Austin for America came off the Longbridge assembly lines in November. By this time in Portugal there were 2,000 Austins in Lisbon alone.

The new A40 caused problems in Bermuda, where 464 of the island's 1,368 cars were Austins. Bermuda's legislation prohibited cars of more than 10hp under the RAC rating system - and the A40 was 10.6hp. In February 1948 the Bermuda House of Assembly voted to raise the limit to 12hp and Austin's distributors, Young, Trott & Co., cabled Longbridge with orders: 85 Devons and

An early production Devon posed at Lower Slaughter in the Cotswolds in November 1947. Later models had slightly bigger headlights with separate side lights mounted beneath them.

Below: Alpine testing of a Dorset prototype with dummy grilles. Production cars were four inches wider. Some of the prototype Dorsets had the smaller 1000cc engine.

Below right: The A40 chassis in October 1947. The bigger A70 which followed was generally similar in layout.

four 10cwt vans on the next boat and a further 50 Devons on the following boat.

Austin immediately shipped 25 cars on the monthly freighter to Bermuda and in addition managed to get the owners of the ss *Planter* to make a special call at the island with a further 50 cars. Then with 25 cars on the high seas and 50 ready to go, the upper house of the Bermuda parliament rescinded the decision to raise the power limits. The outcome was the production of a special version of the A40 for Bermuda in which liners were fitted to the 1200cc engine, reducing its displacement to 1125cc. Suitably modified engines were fitted to the 50 cars booked on the ss *Planter* before she sailed and were retrofitted to the original 25 cars when they arrived in Bermuda. The models for Bermuda had a B suffix added to their type codes.

Throughout 1948 the company kept breaking weekly production records, culminating with a figure of 2,705 during one week in September - of these, 2,066 were exported. Total 1948 exports were worth £20 million.

The first firm signs of rationalisation of Britain's two biggest car builders came in October with the announcement that Austin and Nuffield had agreed to "pool certain of their resources". But this planned co-operation failed and the agreement was soon forgotten.

In the summer of 1949, as the 100,000th A40 was being built, Austin managing director Leonard Lord was warning that there would be no Austins produced for the home market for "a month or two". The 100,000th A40 was awarded to a Longbridge worker, R Wheeler, as part of Austin's employee incentive scheme. Austins were voted the most popular British cars in a South African survey in 1949 and a South African assembly plant was started up by Stanley Motors at Natal Spruit, near Johannesburg, in October. This was in addition to an Austin-owned facility at Blackheath, near Cape Town.

Austins outsold all other cars being imported to Australia in 1949 by a margin of 5,000 vehicles. Cars were being assembled from completely-knocked-down (ckd) kits in Melbourne by the Austin Motor Co. (Australia), formerly Ruskin Motor Body Works, which was taken over by Austin in August 1948, and by companies in Adelaide (All-British Motor House), Brisbane (UK and Dominion Motors), Perth (Winterbottom Motor Co.) and Sydney (Larke, Hoskins). The last-named had produced 10,000 cars by 1950. Assembly in New Zealand was handled by Austin Dis-

> The allocation of steel to the motor industry cannot be considered as at all satisfactory, and the capacity of our industry to earn foreign currency has yet to be fully appreciated.
> - *Leonard Lord, September 1948*

> The A.A. urges members to avoid, as far as possible, the use of headlights in well-lighted streets.
> - *The Light Car, June 1949*

DEVONS IN BUILD

Welders put together the body shell.

Finishing touches being made to completed bodies before they are taken off the track and lifted on to waiting chassis.

The finishing lines in 1948, when production was over 2,500 cars a week. Nearest the camera are Devons, while on the left is a line of Dorsets and on the right a line of Sixteens, now looking just a bit dated. The Dorsets are left-hand-drive models and all the A40s have export stickers in their windscreens.

Since this journal carried out the first Road Test of the then new and unknown Austin A40 early in 1948 a tremendous success has been scored by this model. It has become world famous, is as popular at home as it deserves to be, to an extent limited only by the dictates of the export quota, and in short has established itself firmly as a classic among the smaller cars. When one considers what it gives in relation to its price it is so very good that there is little need to dissect and analyse.
- *introduction to a Devon road test by The Autocar, 19 May 1950.*

tributors (NZ). Nearer to home, there was an assembly line in Eire.

A new Canadian factory was being built in Hamilton, Ontario, on a 29 acre site and with a planned capacity of 500 units a week from 1949, and an assembly plant was established in South America at Buenos Aires, Argentina. There was also an assembly operation in Brazil.

For the benefit of Americans, unused to driving small cars, Austin produced a little booklet with the title "Exciting to drive". It contained such gems of information as: "The first thing to remember when acquiring the feel of the A40 is that it is a four-gear car." Having grasped this piece of information, the new American A40 driver was told that first gear (or "low-low") was an emergency gear and that "the art of driving the A40 to best advantage lies very much in the use of Third Gear". Drivers were encouraged to start in second, to change up to third at 18mph (2,700rpm) and to high (as top was called) at 25-30mph (2,800rpm). The basic message was that the A40 engine needed more revs than the big engines to which Americans were accustomed.

One American who clearly found no difficulty in coping with the A40 was 58-year-old Frank Hocevar of Gary, Indiana. He drove his Dorset coast-to-coast from Los Angeles to New York single-handed. The 3,062 mile run was covered in 57 hours 27 minutes (timed by the Western Union Telegraph) at a record speed of 53.3mph with fuel consumption of 30.6mpg.

Austin publicist Alan Hess cooked up a scheme to attract attention to the Devon, with a plan to run 10,000 miles in 10,000 minutes on the Bonneville salt flats at Utah in the USA, in April 1949. Hess and his colleagues set sail on the liner *Queen Elizabeth*, only to find on arrival at New York that because of unseasonal rain the salt flats were under water. So instead Hess decided to go for endurance records up to 24 hours on the perimeter track of Suffolk County Airfield at Westhampton, Long Island. Driving was to be shared between Hess and Colonel Goldie Gardner.

The track was not ideal. It had sharp corners and although Hess and his team had a go at breaking some stock car records they ended up abandoning the attempt after Gardner had a night time collision with a deer. However the car performed well enough for Austin to use the run to promote the A40 as covering 1,000 miles at an average speed of 65mph and breaking 36 American stock

Cars were delivered by road and by rail. A Devon is pushed on to a train of drive-through wagons in the Longbridge loading bay. Crated cars are stacked on the right. The crates are marked: "Austin. Britain has made it."

Manchester docks, and the *Pacific Stronghold* waits for its load of A40s for the USA in March 1948. Nearest the camera is a Dorset; most of the other cars appear to be Devons, including one actually in the air alongside the warehouses. This was claimed to be a record shipment of British cars - 420 Austins with freight charges exceeding £14,000.

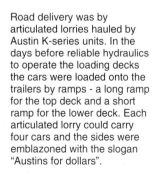

Road delivery was by articulated lorries hauled by Austin K-series units. In the days before reliable hydraulics to operate the loading decks the cars were loaded onto the trailers by ramps - a long ramp for the top deck and a short ramp for the lower deck. Each articulated lorry could carry four cars and the sides were emblazoned with the slogan "Austins for dollars".

car records in the process. After the run Hess drove the damaged Devon from New York to Toronto on a fuel economy drive monitored by the American Automobile Association. Over 514 miles the car averaged 31mph and 39.99mpg (Imperial) which equalled 33.3 miles per US gallon - a figure roughly twice as good as many Americans were used to.

Hess however did eventually achieve his aim and in August 1950 a Devon did the 10,000 miles in 10,000 minutes run at the Montlhery track in France, which was no mean achievement for the car and its team of four drivers. The drivers - Hess, Arthur Fisher, John Walters and Ronald Jeavons - each did three-hour shifts at the wheel.

In actual fact after six days the car was averaging 65.62mph and Hess stopped it for 12 hours to achieve his target 10,000 miles in 10,000 minutes. He justified this decision afterwards: "It may seem strange that so good an average as 65mph plus was sacrificed in this way, but remember '10,000 miles in 10,000 minutes' was the original objective and all Austin's and their associated suppliers' publicity was pre-arranged on this basis and endless complications would have ensued had it been departed from so late in the day. Also, I am (still) convinced that it was a wise move to stop as we did because the magic phrase '10,000 miles in 10,000 minutes' massages the ego of the man in the street who can work out for himself (and his wife!) that it represents 60mph, whereas 10,000 miles in 9,374 minutes means precisely nothing to him."

The A40 was soon developed to include a 10cwt van to replace the old Ten and, announced in September 1948, a factory-built 10cwt pick-up. With it came an A40 Countryman, essentially the van body with windows added to make a metal-bodied estate car. The A40 commercial vehicles shared the front-end pressings, including the doors of the Devon, but had 17in (instead of 16in) wheels which necessitated a bigger cut-out in the wings. They also had lower gear ratios. Early vans had aluminium bodies and spats to enclose the rear wheels; later bodies were of steel and without the spats which hindered wheel-changing. Some commercial bodies were produced by Briggs Motor Bodies.

The commercials were promoted in the USA where to cross the trans-Atlantic language barrier the Countryman was described as the station wagon and the van became the panel delivery. The Devon-style chromed front grille was dropped early in 1951 for a painted pressed metal grille.

Not least of the Devon's attractions is its extreme running economy. There can be very few cars of equal size and performance which give a fuel consumption of nearly 40 m.p.g. under normal conditions. Routine maintenance tasks are simplified by the accessibility of the engine and its components; the smooth lines of the body, besides presenting a handsome appearance, make washing down easier.
- *The Light Car Devon road test, August 1950.*

An early A40 van with fabric roof and Devon-style radiator. The spats over the rear wheels were discontinued on later models.

A 1950 A40 Countryman shows the later lighting arrangement for both commercials and Devons with separate side lights.

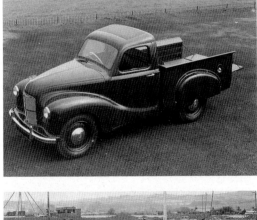

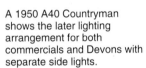

The A40 was also available as a pick-up. This 1948 prototype has only one windscreen wiper.

The A40 chassis was used by specialist builders to provide vehicles such as ice cream vans for Walls. When this A40 was delivered, somewhat unseasonably in December 1949, a family brick cost 1s 6d.

The commercial range was revised in 1951 with the fitment of a pressed steel radiator grille. The original design, shown on this van, did not provide adequate cooling and additional grilles were cut into the bonnet.

A 1953 wooden-bodied left-hand-drive estate car, produced by an unidentified coachbuilder. The rear-hinged rear doors and fabric roof are distinctly old-fashioned features.

The two-door Dorset was short-lived and was dropped from production in October 1949 after less than 16,000 had been built. This compares with Devon production of almost 275,000. Very few Dorsets were sold in the UK and it had in fact been taken off the home market in September 1948.

The open tourer, so redolent of prewar British motoring, had disappeared from Austin's range with the demise of the Eight. A prototype A40 tourer was built in August 1948 to ascertain how many existing body panels could be used, but it did not enter production. However in Australia a large number of A40-based two-door tourers were produced locally from late 1948, ready for the antipodean summer. These were bodied by Austin Motor Co. (formerly Ruskin) of Melbourne and had detachable glass side curtains which could be used with the hood up or down. The boot had special compartments to hold the side screens so that the glass would not break. The Australian tourer was launched at £560 plus sales tax. It was briefly marketed as the Austin Falcon with two-tone paint by Larke, Hoskins, Austin's distributor in Sydney. UK and Dominion Motors in Brisbane also produced a two-tone model which was advertised as the A40 Smart Set Tourer. Detachable glass fibre tops were later made as an accessory for the A40 tourer.

Another open A40 produced in Australia was the Rouseabout, built for UK and Dominion Mo-

tors by Charles Hope. These were door-less Jeep-like vehicles with a canvas roof and a steel-sided wooden-floored load area in the back. Fewer than 100 were built and were used by farmers and newspaper delivery men.

A more common Australian special was the coupé utility, more often known simply as a ute in Australia, or as a pick-up elsewhere. A number of builders produced pick-up bodies in Australia including Charles Hope in Brisbane and Larke, Hoskins in Sydney. Most stylish of the range was Larke, Hoskins' Hi-Lite which had a curved perspex rear window on the cab (described as an Astro-type rear light).

The first Devons had small 5in headlamps with integral side lights. But a change in US lighting requirements saw these being replaced in December 1948 by bigger 7in headlamps with separate side lights underneath.

A Mark II Devon was introduced in May 1949. This was essentially a no-frills model for export. It had a bench front seat (in place of twin seats), leathercloth trim instead of genuine leather and it lacked bumper over-riders. These changes cut the ex-works price from £365 to £328. It had a higher back axle ratio and different gear box ratios too. Extras listed for the Mark II were sunshine roof (£3 0s 6d), heater (5 guineas), trafficators (£3 15s) and a tyre and tube for the spare wheel (£4 2s 6d). Few were sold.

It remains lively, getting up into the forties quickly with only moderate use of the gears from rest, and on an average English journey, complicated by built-up areas, traffic and a multitude of bends, it is almost as fast as any car short of the top-performance class. The engine is delightfully smooth and the only time when it is felt at all is in a slight roughness noticeable on the overrun - that is, when the throttle pedal is released to decelerate.
- *The Autocar Devon road test, 19 May 1950.*

There was no factory-built open car in Austin's early postwar range. This prototype A40 tourer was completed in August 1948 but was not put into production. The use of the old Eight-style wheels is surprising.

A Dutch builder produced this stylish cabriolet on an A40 in 1949.

It was left to the Australians to develop an A40 tourer. The central line in this shot of Dominion Motors, Brisbane, in November 1949 includes five tourers. It was taken to mark the production of 1,000 Austins in one month by Dominion.

From September 1949 opening front quarter lights were fitted to all Devons, responding to criticism of inadequate ventilation. The rear axle ratio was also changed from 5.43 to 5.14 which made for slightly more relaxed high-speed cruising, taking the cruising speed up from the 50-55mph range to 55-60mph.

By mid-1950 Austin was claiming to have exported 10,000 vehicles to Belgium since the end of the war. The company also claimed its 250,000th postwar export - a Devon - which was shipped to the New York motor show in March before being delivered to Australia later in the year.

The 250,000th A40 was produced in November 1950, at which time production was running at the rate of 450 a day. Of the 250,000, 79 per cent had been exported and only 21 per cent - 52,500 cars - supplied to the home market. In a little over three years the company had earned $70 million from US exports and the A40 was identified as the product which had earned more dollars for Britain than any other one-make commodity. The Devon marked as export number 250,000 carried a silver plate to mark the milestone. Britain was now the world's biggest exporter, and Austin was playing its part in this achievement

In August 1951, just six months before production was to end, a revised version of the Devon appeared with column gear change, a new cen-

trally-located instrument panel, different steering wheel and full hydraulic brakes to replace the original Girling hydro-mechanical system. The Devon was coming under attack from new models from Austin's competitors - notably Ford's Consul and Morris's Minor - but the August 1951 improvements appear to have been linked to changes in chassis production which anticipated the launch in the spring of 1952 of the new Somerset. The Somerset's chassis, which differed little from that of the Devon, had a column gear change and hydraulic brakes, and the Devon's new instruments were those which were to appear on the Somerset. The revised Devon was exhibited at the 1951 Earls Court Motor Show.

Devon production ceased in February 1952, at which time Austin was claiming to have built 344,000 A40s, of which 77 per cent had been exported to earn £88 million for Britain. The Devon-based van, pick-up and Countryman continued in production. The new pressed-steel radiator grille fitted from May 1951 had a smaller intake area and was found to offer inadequate cooling in warm climates. From August 1951 it was revised to incorporate additional louvres on the leading edge of the bonnet. The final revision to the commercial range was the installation from September 1954 of the new BMC B-series 1200cc engine.

Production ceased late in 1956. The replacement was the unitary construction A50 van.

Sketches for bodies suitable for the A40.

The Mark II Devon was a no-frills export model. Unusually this example had a roof-mounted windscreen wiper.

The original Devon interior with floor-mounted gearchange and instruments located directly ahead of the driver.

An Australian coupé utility, the A40-based Hi-Lite with Astro-type wrap-round rear window.

By July 1948 Austin had exported 100,000 cars. They went to the following territories:	
Western Europe	13,500
Australia	9,400
USA	8,000
South Africa	6,600
South America	6,500*
New Zealand	6,200
India and Pakistan	5,700
Spain and Portugal	5,200
Scandinavia and Finland	5,100
Eire	5,000
Canada	4,700
South East Asia	4,700
Middle East (Turkey, Iran)	3,000
West Indies	3,000
East Africa	2,500
Ceylon	2,000
West Africa	1,900
China	1,100
Egypt	1,000
Central America	600
North Africa	300
Others	4,000

* including 2,000 in Argentina and 1,000 in Uruguay.

The big cars

THE LAUNCH OF the Devon and Dorset overshadowed another new Austin project which had first appeared earlier in 1947, the A125 Sheerline. This was Austin's foray into a market which was effectively to disappear in postwar Britain, the large luxury saloon. The A125 was an imposing car. It was dubbed the poor man's Bentley, but with the 3993cc six-cylinder K-series truck engine returning fuel economy of around 17mpg it was by no means a car for someone with limited financial resources. It was originally developed as the Austin 25 and launched in February 1947 as the A110 with the smaller 3.5-litre version of the truck engine. The decision to use the 4-litre engine was taken in November. The steel-bodied Sheerline was 16ft long and weighed 37cwt.

Even more luxurious was the A135 Princess, launched at the March 1947 Geneva Motor Show as the 3.5-litre A120. Built on the same chassis as the Sheerline, the Princess had stylish wood-framed aluminium bodywork by Austin's newly-acquired Vanden Plas subsidiary in Kingsbury, North London. A Princess limousine with division behind the driver followed in December 1948.

A long-wheelbase Sheerline appeared in October 1949 and a long-wheelbase Princess followed in October 1952, ultimately replacing the long-wheelbase Sheerline which was discontinued in October 1953. The Princess had appeared in MkII form in October 1950 with a restyled rear door and window. The standard wheelbase Sheerline was dropped in August 1954, but the Princess, by this time largely a car for wedding and funeral hire businesses, continued - indeed with various updates it was to survive until 1968.

Although both models used the same engine,

the original Princess had three SU carburettors compared with a single Stromberg on the Sheerline; the triple carburettor arrangement on the Princess soon became an option. To stop these heavy cars Austin fitted Lockheed hydraulic brakes. A hydraulic jacking system was fitted too. The chassis was used as a base for coachbuilt hearse and ambulance bodies and for this use was fitted with a lower ratio rear axle which was also specified for the Sheerline limousine. A small number of long-wheelbase A135s had landaulette bodywork by Vanden Plas with an opening hood over the rear seats.

Production of the A125 and A135 peaked at a creditable 3,000-plus in 1949-50, but three years later the figure had dropped below 300 and that was generally where it stayed for the remainder of the big car's production life.

The new cars which were launched in 1947, and most subsequent Austins until the 1959 Mini Seven, featured a new bonnet motif, a forward-leaning A with wing-like speed lines flowing back from it, the so-called flying-A. This stylish motif was used on trucks too, as well as on the company's advertising literature and on agents' premises. It was designed by Austin's talented Italian-born stylist, Dick Burzi.

With the launch of the A40 and the A125, Austin was the first major British manufacturer to abandon side-valve engines, a fact which it frequently used to promote the modernity of its cars. In making this point Austin clearly discounted American-owned Vauxhall, all of whose postwar cars had overhead valve engines - but arch-rivals Morris used side-valve engines in the Oxford until 1954, Hillman in the Minx till 1955 while Ford produced a side-valve Anglia until 1959.

This top-of-the-range Austin model is aimed at providing luxury rather than just good standards of comfort. Extensive trial of the latest model has served to confirm in no uncertain fashion that the Princess saloon has a definite niche among the larger cars. It is big but not unwieldy - it will fit, rather surprisingly, into a not exceptionally long private garage - and the overhead-valve engine gives a power output of an order that makes this extensively equipped car a very satisfactory means of long-distance conveyance.
- The Autocar road test of a Princess II, 1952.

Before adopting model numbers based on brake horse power, Austin got as far as producing publicity material for its range of big postwar saloons which described the Sheerline as the Austin 25.

Production models appeared as the A120 and then as the A125 when the engine was increased in size and power. The flowing wing lines were an Austin hallmark, developed by stylist Dick Burzi. The huge P100 headlamps gave the Sheerline an imposing appearance. This is an early vehicle, photographed in October 1946, five months before the model was launched. The radio aerial is just visible under the driver's door.

The long-wheelbase A125.

The Vanden Plas Princess had sleek lines. The original version (*left*) had restricted vision from the rear seats. This was addressed by the Princess II (*right*) with a new rear door incorporating a bigger window.

Pedal cars

IN 1946 A SMALL team at Austin set to work to design a children's pedal car. It was developed with as much secrecy as any real car and was based on the Austin Eight. A prototype was built and was followed by a second car, modelled on a prewar Austin Seven Special.

Production of the pedal-powered racing car for children was put into production in a new Austin-owned factory in South Wales in 1949, with target output of 100 a week. The factory at Pengam, Bargoed, employed men suffering from miner's pneumoconiosis and started up with 55 former miners no longer able to work underground.

The racing car was dubbed the Pathfinder Special, and it was soon joined at the Austin Junior Car Factory by a pretty roadster based loosely on the A40 Devon styling. The Pathfinder Special was 5ft 3in long and weighed 75lbs; the roadster, known as the J40, was 5ft 0in long and weighed 95lbs - which clearly required rather more pedal power from little legs.

The cars were made using scrap material left over from building real Austins and the main body pressings were produced at Longbridge and shipped to Pengam for assembly, painting and trimming. The J40 - also known as the Joy car - had battery-operated horn and headlamps and initially sold for £34 8s; the Pathfinder Special sold for £25 10s 8d.

Pathfinder production ceased in July 1950 after a 12 month run, but the J40 enjoyed a long production run and secured export business too. A total of 32,098 J40s was built; the last one was completed in September 1971.

The prototype pedal car, JOY 1. The girl is Marcia, the eight-year-old daughter of designer Alfred Ash, the only member of the pedal car design team with a child of the right age. She road-tested the prototype in Longbridge works and revealed a problem with brake noise and the weight of the car. A second prototype, JOY 2 based on the A40 Devon was then built.

Pathfinder pedal cars take shape in South Wales in 1949.

The production version of the popular J40 pedal car, also built in South Wales, looked like a scaled-down Devon. It enjoyed a remarkable 22 year production run. Many were used for fairground rides.

One thing strikes me very forcibly. These beautifully made models must not be regarded merely as toys. They provide a fine training ground for the driver of the future: "road" sense, steering, reversing and all the rest. He'll be a lucky youngster who enjoys his earliest training on anything so soundly and scientifically constructed.
- *columnist in The Light Car, April 1948.*

1948: The Hampshire arrives

THE REPLACEMENT FOR the Sixteen, a postwar car with a prewar look, was announced in September 1948 and carried on the new theme of county names started with the Devon and Dorset. The new car was the A70 Hampshire and it used the same 67bhp 2199cc engine and gearbox as the Sixteen (but with different gear ratios) in a new chassis with independent front suspension. It had a column-mounted gear-change, a feature which would appear on subsequent Counties cars. Girling hydro-mechanical brakes were fitted.

The Hampshire was priced at £609 13s 11d, compared with £684 7s 3d for the Sixteen (which had just been reduced in price from £709 18s 4d). At the Hampshire's launch Leonard Lord indicated that it was to be "considered as additional to the present type Sixteen" - but its arrival spelt the end of the last of the old-style Austins and the Sixteen was taken out of production in 1949.

The four-door saloon body was of what was still described as a six light design and it looked like a scaled-up Devon. The rear wheels were enclosed by detachable spats to emphasise the car's flowing lines. The Hampshire was lighter than the Sixteen by about 10 per cent, weighing

24cwt instead of 26.5cwt. A Countryman wooden-bodied estate car variant was launched in January 1950, and the Hampshire chassis/scuttle (but with the wheelbase lengthened from 8ft to 8ft 7.5in) was also used for factory-built pick-ups and coach-built vans and estate cars. At least two convertibles were also built.

A Hampshire hit the headlines at the end of 1948 when it was driven from Britain to Cape Town in 24 days, knocking an incredible eight days off the previous best journey time. Driven by Ralph Sleigh and Peter Jopling, it also broke the Algiers to Cape Town record by more than three days. The car had auxiliary fuel tanks mounted on the roof and was carrying half a ton of equipment. The Hampshire's record fell in 1952 to a Hillman Minx which was driven from London to Cape Town in just under 22 days.

The Hampshire was short-lived, being replaced after a little over two years by the A70 Hereford which used a totally new body on the same chassis but with the rear springs rearranged to give a 3in longer wheelbase. Towards the end of its production the Hampshire acquired swivelling front quarter lights, as had the Devon.

During its life 35,000 Hampshires were built.

The new cars are exceedingly attractive, if the things that matter most are a smart but not exaggerated modern appearance, really lively performance, refinement of running, comprehensive equipment, smart interior trim, and a favourable ratio of power to weight, topped with the Austin reputation for dependability.
- The Autocar, 10 September 1948, on the launch of the A70 Hampshire and A90 Atlantic.

By July 1947 a full-size wooden model of a new Sixteen had been completed in the experimental shop. The inboard mounted headlamps and the general appearance of the radiator grille were carried over to the production model, but little else was. Note that one side of the car shows a six-light (three window) design while the other is a four-light (two windows).

Early ideas for a Sixteen replacement were taking shape by November 1946. This clay model shows some of the features which would appear on the new A70: flowing wings, no running boards and the protruding boot line.

When the A70 Hampshire appeared in September 1948 it looked very much like a big Devon. Both cars used the same radiator grille - but shared nothing else.

A 1949 Hampshire shooting brake with traditional wooden bodywork. The interior view shows the wooden ceiling.

A smart steel-bodied estate car by Hawson on an A70. This vehicle had an unusual three-door layout with two doors on the passenger side, but only the driver's door on the other side. It was built in 1950.

Prices: Austin and the competition, October 1949			
	£	s	d
Ford Prefect	371	6	1
Vauxhall Wyvern	479	18	4
A40 Devon	501	12	10
Hillman Minx	505	9	5
Morris Oxford	546	7	3
Standard Vanguard	594	18	4
A70 Hampshire	648	11	8
Morris Six	671	11	8
Ford V8 Pilot	748	5	0
Jowett Javelin	761	0	7

The A70 pick-up with framework for a canvas tilt.

The 1950 Amsterdam show with ten cars on display, including the sectioned Atlantic which was the centrepiece of Austin's stand at the previous autumn's Earls Court Show. Of most interest are the two unusual A70 Hampshire convertibles - one with the hood up in the left foreground and the other with the hood down on the right of the stand.

The A70 was used as a base for coachbuilt bodies. Walls specified this ice cream van body in 1950. The A70's greater load capacity was presumably used in areas where more ice cream was consumed than those served by the A40 van illustrated on page 15.

A comprehensive tool kit was fitted in the Hampshire's boot lid.

Austin's export packing department putting a dusty A70 Hampshire in a box. The wheels have been removed and are mounted on the box ends, presumably to minimise the size of the box and thus cut shipping costs.

Many vehicles were still shipped without being boxed. A40s and a Sheerline are loaded at Liverpool for Australia in November 1949. Under the crane a crated car is ready to be lifted. The London-registered Hampshire in the foreground was not being shipped and shows the model's six-light design and rear wheel spats.

Launch of a dollar earner

AUSTIN'S MOST DARING postwar car was the A90 Atlantic, a stylish two-door convertible aimed fairly and squarely at the American market. The Atlantic used the 8ft wheelbase A70 chassis and was powered by an 88bhp version of the A70 engine, bored out to 2660cc and fitted with twin SU carburettors. Bigger brakes and a larger clutch were fitted to cope with the A90's increased power. Coincidentally this ultra-modern looking high-speed tourer appeared in the year when the British government passed the Special Roads Act which laid the foundation for building motorways - although ten years were to pass before any were actually built.

The convertible with a power-operated hood and windows was announced in September 1948 and shown at the October Earls Court Motor Show, along with the new A70 Hampshire. This was the first postwar motor show and although there was a waiting list for new cars it attracted 562,000 visitors at 5s a head before 5pm and 2s 6d after 5pm. Austin, who had the Atlantic on a revolving turntable, handed out 170,000 brochures. The Atlantic had a selling price of £952 13s 11d but within six months this was reduced to £824 18s 4d. It was also available with a manually operated hood for £786 11s 8d. Series production started in February 1949.

A hardtop Atlantic was announced 12 months after the convertible, selling for £888 16s 1d, and it appeared at the 1949 Motor Show. Production started in January 1950. The only mechanical difference between the hardtop and the convertible was the fitment of a different axle ratio which reduced its top speed.

The Atlantic had flowing lines and was the first British postwar production car to abandon any semblance of a conventional radiator grille. Chrome trim strips ran up the centre of the bonnet and boot - apeing contemporary American practice - and the car had an unusually large glass area with curved screens front and rear. The centre section of the three-piece rear window on the saloon could be opened - it wound down into a compartment in the boot. Commented *The Autocar*: "Striking but not gaudy is the considered verdict on the A90's appearance, which is apt to grow on one."

The Atlantic also had what were described in 1948 as "winking type" indicators which operated through the side and tail lamps, although home market Atlantics appeared with conventional semaphore arm indicators. Flashing trafficators were not legal in Britain until 1954.

It was a bold car. But it failed to sell in significant numbers. Although quite big by British standards, it was a small car in the USA and American motorists could - and did - buy home produced Chevrolets and Plymouths which of-

The Atlantic can truthfully be described as the most striking car which has ever emerged from the Longbridge factory. Its coachwork represents a complete departure from previous Austin models, and the bold, downward sweep of the bonnet, flowing wings, flared into the body sides, and sloping tail terminating in a massive bumper, which is curved round to meet the chromium protective strips along the base of the body, all have a distinct suggestion of the specialized Italian creations which have met with such a favourable reception in all parts of the world.
- *The Motor, 15 September 1948*

Leonard Lord took a personal interest in styling. An Atlantic model comes under scrutiny with Dick Burzi.

This 16hp sports prototype was completed early in 1948, before the launch in November of the A90 Atlantic. The body is little different from production A90s apart from the two-piece windscreen and the unusual foot-operated door control, a pedal just visible inset into the bright rubbing strip on the bottom of the door.

fered comparable performance and more interior space for the same sort of price. In the end American sales were disappointing and the UK proved to be the Atlantic's best market.

An Atlantic convertible was sent to the Indianapolis race track in April 1949 where under a team piloted by Austin's Alan Hess it broke a long list of records: 63 in all, some of which remain unbroken 40-plus years on. Driven by Hess, Dennis Buckley and Charles Goodacre, the Atlantic covered 11,850 miles in seven days and nights, using 694 gallons of fuel. This, Hess noted in his book *The Indianapolis Records*, was the equivalent of 13 years basic petrol ration in austere postwar Britain.

Creditable as the Atlantic's performance was, Austin did indulge in some subterfuge, initially running the car with an engine with an aluminium block and head. This saved weight, but the engine was damaged when after tappet adjustment too much pressure was applied to studs in the head. A standard engine was fitted to complete the run. The event was an attention-grabber on both sides of the Atlantic and *The Indianapolis Times* on 6 April had as its front page headline: "Tiny Austin Tackles 1939 Hudson Speedway Record".

The run may have created interest but it failed to create sales. After the publicity had died down Leonard Lord is reported to have said that the Indianapolis run did not create one extra sale. The

dismal American sales figures for the car suggest he was right and the Atlantic was withdrawn in September 1952 after fewer than 8,000 had been built. Convertible production had actually halted at the end of 1950. When production ceased the men on the Atlantic line at Longbridge were sacked, precipitating a 12 week strike which was the biggest stoppage the British motor industry had yet experienced.

Coachbuilders E D Abbott of Farnham, recognising that the Atlantic had not been a roaring success, were in 1954 offering wooden-framed estate car conversions of the model. It was a bold idea, but one which found few takers.

The A90 engine lived on as the power unit for the original Healey 100 sports car, launched at the 1952 Motor Show, and soon adopted by Austin as the Austin-Healey 100.

The Atlantic might not have been the runaway success which Austin had hoped for, but thanks to the Devon, 1949 was a record year for the company with production reaching 157,628 vehicles. In one week in September it produced 3,114 vehicles which it claimed as a record for any British motor manufacturer. Exports in the 12 months to July 1949 totalled 76,000 vehicles worth £26 million.

In 1949 the Swiss importer of Austins reported that they had sold their 5,000th postwar British car - and that 3,500 of them had been Austins.

While the earlier convertible model settled down to a natural cruising speed of just over 70 m.p.h., I found that the lower-geared saloon seemed at its best around 65 m.p.h. Against this must be set the fact that its hill-climbing capabilities on top gear have undoubtedly been improved.
- *Country Life road test, 25 May 1951*

At the 1949 Motor Show the centrepiece of Austin's display was a striking cutaway of the Atlantic hardtop.

The chrome strips on the Atlantic bonnet were repeated on the boot. It was a distinctive and stylish car from any angle.

No significant changes were made to the Atlantic during its short production run, but a restyling exercise was carried out in the summer of 1950 which saw a lengthened American-looking tail being grafted on to a convertible.

Alan Hess (second from the
left) and his team (including
George Coates, far right) pose
before loading the Indianapolis
record-breaking Atlantic on the
Queen Mary.

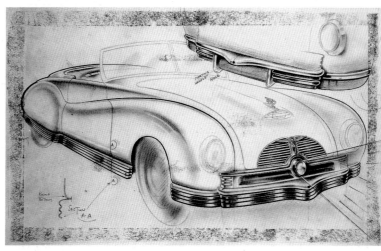

Hawaiian motoring statistics for
1951 reflect on the successful
year of British car exports. The
number of Austins sold in Hono-
lulu was exceeded only by
Studebakers, and Hillman, Morris and M.G. were well up in the
list.
- *The Autocar, 18 April 1952*

A sketch for the development
of the Atlantic with new wing
line, improved cooling for the
radiator, and a two-piece split
windscreen.

Taxi!

AUSTIN'S DOMINANT POSITION as a major builder of
taxicabs to meet the tough regulations laid down
by London's Metropolitan Police was secured
with the launch in June 1948 of the new FX3. This
was based on the A70 Hampshire chassis but with
a much longer wheelbase of 9ft 2.5in and used the
same 2199cc petrol engine but derated to 52bhp. It
also had a conventional front axle with revised
steering to give a tight turning circle - only 25ft
compared with the Hampshire's 39ft.

The FX3, like earlier London taxis, had a full-
width windscreen but only a half-width driver's
cab; the area on the driver's left was designed for
the carriage of bulky items of luggage. A hire car
variant, the FL1, was introduced at the same time
and had a conventional full-width driving compartment with doors on both sides. The FL1 had a
chrome radiator grille. Diesel power did not appear in both models until 1954, although from the
autumn of 1953 Perkins was offering diesel con-
version packs for £280.

Bodies for the FX3 and FL1 were built in
Coventry by Carbodies and the chassis was also
used for some specialist van applications, most
notably by London newspaper publishers who
appreciated the model's manoeuvrability. The chassis with part-built cab cost £680 9s 5d; the complete taxi was £993 11s 8d.

Austin's sales brochure claimed that over 70
per cent of London's taxis were Austins. And the
company quoted a satisfied cabbie making a claim
which would have led to him being lynched in later
decades: "I find that people seem to prefer the
Austin taxi. On occasions they have pulled me out

of the middle of the rank because they know the
Austin cab is fast and comfortable and it looks
smart."

Small numbers of taxis were exported, notably
to the USA and to Spain, where a fleet was operated in Madrid. The FX3 was replaced by the long-
lived FX4 in 1958.

The taxi range had limited
export appeal. This is an FL1
hire car in New York in 1949.

The classic London taxi, an
FX3 outside Buckingham
Palace in 1950. At this stage
all FX3s were petrol-engined.

Truck progress

THE AUSTIN TRUCK range was updated in 1949 with the launch of the Loadstar which, with its generously curved front wings, bore a strong family resemblance to the new generation of cars under development. The Loadstar was in effect a re-cabbed K2/K4 and included such unheard of luxuries as an optional cab heater. The cab was wider and offered room for a three-man crew.

The Loadstar name was quietly dropped when it was discovered that it was used by a US truck builder but the models remained in production at Longbridge until 1954, and the general styling continued on BMC and even on British Leyland trucks, built at the former BMC Bathgate factory, until the 1970s.

We who drive private cars can learn much from long-distance lorry drivers - amongst other things, the fact that head lamps are superfluous on a clear night when the moon is at the full. On one such night not so long ago, I followed their example and found that, except at quite high cruising speeds, I got along just as easily with only side lights in use.

I found, too, that a familiar and not very inspiring route took on a quite unexpected and sightly theatrical beauty.

- columnist in The Light Car, October 1949.

Left: New cabs transformed the appearance of Austin's lorries, although the mechanical components underneath were largely unchanged. This is a 5 ton tipper demonstrating the three-man cab.

Below: A cab is lowered onto a chassis.

Below: A 5 ton Austin K fitted with a racing car transporter body for British Racing Motors, better known as BRM.

Below, left: The Loadstar had a full-width cab and flowing wings which anticipated the styling of the next generation of Austin cars. This one from Austin's own fleet is carrying parts for delivery to Turkey in the summer of 1950.

Below, right: A K-series fire engine being prepared for delivery to the Brussels commercial vehicle show in January 1952.

Showrooms, parts and servicing

T Startin Jnr Ltd. was a Birmingham-based Austin distributor whose premises were thought impressive enough to receive the attention of Longbridge's photographers. The exterior view of the showroom has an A40 pick-up in Austin service livery parked outside. Visible in the showroom are an A40 Sports and a Somerset coupé. There are still tram tracks in the roadway - this photograph was taken in July 1953, the month when the city's last trams were replaced by motorbuses.

Inside Startin's showroom, from right to left, an A70 Hereford, an A40 pick-up, an A40 van and an A70 Countryman. The bench seat on the left is a display of car seat covers by Karobes of Leamington Spa.

Startin's parts department (on the right of the showroom in the exterior view). The neat stack of boxes on the end of the counter are described on the board on the floor which reads: "Genuine Austin carton packed replacement parts. Cartoned packed parts are protected against damage and the effects of varying climates and retain their factory condition." Karobes have another seat cover display at the far end of the counter.

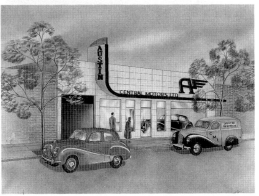

Later in 1953 Austin came up with idealised designs for agents' premises, setting out a modern image. A fictional Central Motors showroom shows the frontage, while inside a customer waiting room gives views of the service area - an advanced concept for the time.

1950: Hereford ousts Hampshire

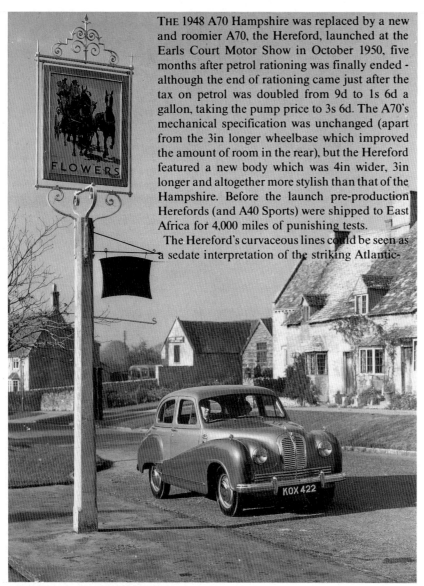

THE 1948 A70 Hampshire was replaced by a new and roomier A70, the Hereford, launched at the Earls Court Motor Show in October 1950, five months after petrol rationing was finally ended - although the end of rationing came just after the tax on petrol was doubled from 9d to 1s 6d a gallon, taking the pump price to 3s 6d. The A70's mechanical specification was unchanged (apart from the 3in longer wheelbase which improved the amount of room in the rear), but the Hereford featured a new body which was 4in wider, 3in longer and altogether more stylish than that of the Hampshire. Before the launch pre-production Herefords (and A40 Sports) were shipped to East Africa for 4,000 miles of punishing tests.

The Hereford's curvaceous lines could be seen as a sedate interpretation of the striking Atlantic-

in particular the front wing line, flowing back towards the rear wheelarch, echoed one of the key styling features of the Atlantic. It had curved front and rear windows. New push-button door handles were fitted.

The road tester for *The Light Car* was suitably impressed, saying: "Not only does the Hereford provide an unusual degree of comfort and spaciousness, but it gives performance of a very high order." Fuel consumption averaged 30mpg, although it dropped to 22mpg when the car was driven hard. The Hereford sold for £738 0s 7d.

New car supplies were still restricted and the British Motor Trade Association's covenant system was tightened up. From December 1950 any buyer of a new car had to keep it two years instead of one and had to complete a questionnaire giving

By July 1950 the new A70 - to appear as the Hereford - was pretty well ready with only detail differences from the final production car. The side windows lack opening quarter lights and the Austin of England scroll is on the door instead of the bonnet side. The radiator grille badge would change and the three strips on the bonnet side would be replaced by an oval device - but these details aside this prototype was close to the final product.

The A70 Hereford was one of Austin's most attractive postwar cars. Roomier than the Hampshire which it replaced, its appearance was altogether more exuberant at a time when most other makers were moving towards sober slab-sided models. The Coach & Horses pub sign offers accommodation for motorists.

No sooner had the A70 Hampshire been launched than its replacement was being styled. This March 1949 view of a full-size mock-up illustrates what would have been a most attractive car using many of the Atlantic's styling features. A prototype Somerset clay model is in the background - three years before its public appearance.

The A70 coupé was a rare model indeed, with only 266 being built. One stands outside the new Car Assembly Building in April 1951. The bodywork was by Carbodies of Coventry.

While the smaller A40 commercials retained the Devon-style front end after the introduction of the Somerset, the larger A70 commercials adopted the new Hereford style when the Hampshire was replaced. This is a Hereford-based pick-up.

details of any new cars which he had bought and sold since 1946. Used cars were still appreciating in value. In 1951 a used Hampshire could sell for between £1,245 and £1,465 - more than double the new price in 1949. The revised covenant did allow that where someone felt they had to sell their car within the two year period the BMTA would arrange for its repurchase less an allowance for wear and tear.

In 1951 a Hereford and a Hampshire were the only two British cars among 26 entered in the punishing 500km Luanda rally in Angola. They finished first and third.

The Hereford had a longer production life than the Hampshire which it replaced, surviving until October 1954. Most were standard four-door saloons, but until 1952 a two-door convertible was offered (built by Carbodies) and from June 1951 there was also a wooden-bodied Countryman estate car which was built for Austin by Papworth

Industries of Cambridge, although other coachbuilders also bodied the A70 to special order. The convertible, described by Austin as a coupé, had a leathercloth hood which could be folded back to what was known as the De Ville position, leaving just the two front seats exposed to the sun. It could also, of course, be retracted into a well behind the rear seat. Power operation was available as an option. Only 266 Hereford coupés were built of which 180 were for the home market and 86 for export.

Like the Hampshire before it, the Hereford chassis/scuttle was used as the basis for coach-built vans and factory-produced 15cwt pick-ups. The A70 pick-up had a bigger clutch (9in instead of 8in on the saloon) and was lower geared. It ran on 17in wheels, an inch bigger than the saloon, and the wheelbase was extended by 4.5in to 8ft 7.5in.

The last of the Herefords was built in 1954. Its replacement was the totally new six-cylinder A90 Westminster.

At night, the phenomenon of bright lights producing a double image in the curved screen is in evidence in mild form and another detail fault is that the roof light is so dim that the amber-tinted plastic cover had to be removed for map reading; as the car was not ours, we replaced it.
- *The Motor, Hereford road test, 2 May 1951.*

Before abandoning curves, Austin gave consideration to an A70 facelift. This clay model was photographed in November 1952 and features a grille with wavy mesh which would become a feature of the next generation of Austins, albeit not on this style of body.

In 1950 a fleet of cars was tested in East Africa. A Hereford, with ventilation louvres on the bonnet side just ahead of the doors, illustrates the punishing conditions - high temperatures and poor roads.

The A70 Countryman (left), last in a line of wooden-bodied Austin estate cars.

Alternative estate car bodies for the Hereford. The stylish all metal body with sweeping window line (*right*) was apparently produced by Jensen. It is dated January 1953 and is a left-hand-drive car. The slightly more austere body by Hawson (*below, left*) used the same doors. This is a 1952 model and has the earlier style of wing-mounted side lights. It carries export stickers in the windows. A rather less happy effort from Frank Grounds is based on the A70 pick-up with a fabric and wood superstructure added to the pick-up's metal body. This, too, carries an export label.

A40 Sports

THE A40 DEVON/DORSET was not available from the factory as an open tourer and this gap in the Austin range was plugged in the autumn of 1950 with the launch of the A40 Sports.

This used the A40's 1200cc engine but fitted with twin SU carburettors to boost power to 46bhp, which even by 1950s standards sounds barely enough to justify the appellation 'Sports'. But Sports is what Austin called their new four-seat tourer. In fairness, an *Autocar* road test in 1951 recorded a 0-60mph time of 27.4 seconds for the Sports - a handsome improvement on the 45.6 seconds which took a Devon to reach the same speed. The centre section of the A40 chassis was boxed and strengthened to provide the extra torsional rigidity needed for the open sports body.

It bore no resemblance to any other car in the Austin family, having an aluminium body which was designed and built by Jensen in West Bromwich - and which looked like a scaled-down version of Jensen's Interceptor. *The Light Car* description of the Sports said "The lines are most pleasing. They are of the Italian school, of clean envelope form, not only decorative but practical."

Indeed, *The Light Car* waxed quite lyrical about the car. Its seats were "unusually comfortable" and it was "a delightful little car which one likes instinctively, and the more one drives it, the more one likes it." The Sports sold for £818 3s 4d. The Sports was not the only link between Austin and Jensen. The prestigious Interceptor was powered by the 3993cc six-cylinder Austin engine used in the Sheerline. And at the other end of Jensen's range the utilitarian Jentug truck, designed for moving goods around warehouses and factory yards, used the 1200cc A40 engine. Jensen also produced one special body for an Atlantic.

To win a bet with Leonard Lord - for the princely sum of half-a-crown - Alan Hess organised a 'Round-the-world in 30 days' drive for an A40 Sports in June 1951, working with KLM, whose Skymaster DC4 aircraft carried the car over water. The trip was actually completed in just 21 days during which the car went through Europe via France, Switzerland, Italy, Lebanon, Syria, and Trans-Jordan to Iraq and India, drove across the United States and into Canada, and was then flown back from Montreal to Prestwick. Pye telecommunications equipment was carried to keep the car in touch with the plane.

The car with its team of four drivers (Alan Hess, Ralph Sleigh, Ronald Jeavons and George Coates) had to average 440 miles a day and covered 10,000 miles, much of it in fairly inhospitable territory: the temperature at Basra in the Persian Gulf was a searing 160 degrees, only three days after the car had been coping with snow on the Simplon Pass on its way from Switzerland to Italy. It started from London Airport at Heath Row (as it was then described) on 1 June, returning there on 22 June. It was then driven, within an AA motor-bike escort, to the Festival of Britain on the south bank of the River Thames. Fuel consumption for the trip averaged out at 29mpg. Oil consumption was in excess of 5,000mpg.

To promote the event Universal News showed newsreel film of the run in cinemas throughout the country and ran a competition with a £300 first prize. Entrants had to calculate the A40 Sports' actual running time on the trip and the winner, a 16-year-old patron of the Viking Cinema in Largs, came closest with 4 days, 4 hours, 49 minutes and 49 seconds. He was 31 seconds out.

In August 1951 the Sports, like the Devon, was revised with a column gear change and new instruments and in this form continued until the spring of 1953 when it was withdrawn from the market after just over 4,000 had been built. It had effectively been made redundant by a convertible version of Austin's new A40, the Somerset.

In these days of preparation, however, no country presented such problems as India. There were two main reasons. The first was that the only way to get the car across the mile-wide River Sone at Dehri was by railway truck. One train runs each day at ten a.m. No matter how I amended my schedule it was impossible to get the car to Dehri before ten p.m. - and plainly we could not afford to waste twelve hours there. With the help of the Company's representative in India, Colonel Pratt, I finally overcame this difficulty. We arranged that a special engine should wait with steam up to haul a solitary wagon over the bridge the moment the Austin reached it.

Secondly, no car had ever come to India by air, and officialdom could not think how to deal with the situation.
- Alan Hess on taking the A40 Sports round the world in 21 days.

An A40 Sports, seen here attracting attention in a remote East African village during the 1950 testing.

The new Car Assembly Building in May 1952 with an A40 Sports. It was available only as a convertible.

The A40 Sports bore no resemblance to the rest of the Austin range and was in effect a scaled-down Jensen Interceptor. Jensen built the aluminum body.

The round-the-world A40 Sports was displayed by KLM in their Amsterdam offices.

The Jensen-built A40 Sports body was tried with a mesh grille before being launched (above, right). An alternative bonnet layout was tried too, with a much smaller opening section which had concealed hinges and a Devon type boot handle to open it.

A useful performance is available. Acceleration from the low speeds is not startling, but is more than adequate, and the rate is unusually well maintained, for the size of the engine, into the region of 50 m.p.h. and above. It can be cruised at around 60 m.p.h. - not, it is true, without noise - and it can do better than 75 m.p.h. genuine speed.
- *from The Autocar road test of an A40 Sports*

Prices: October 1951	£	s	d
A40 Devon	685	18	11
A40 Devon (sliding head)	690	12	3
A40 Sports	880	7	9
A70 Hereford	941	1	1
A70 Hereford (sliding head)	955	1	1
A70 Hereford coupé	1174	7	9
A70 Hereford coupé (power-operated head)	1207	1	1
A90 Sports Saloon	1378	3	4
A125 Sheerline Saloon	2183	18	10
A125 Sheerline Limousine	2397	1	1
A135 Princess Saloon	2649	1	1
A135 Princess Limousine	2852	16	8

1951: a new Seven is launched

THE POPULAR PREWAR Seven had been replaced in 1939 by the Eight which had in turn been replaced by the A40 Devon and Dorset in 1947. The A40 was an altogether bigger - and more expensive - car than the Eight and it left Austin without a real economy car in its range. With exports as the main priority this was not really a problem.

The company was aware of the impending gap as early as 1946 and an attractive Seven mock-up was completed that year, with more than a hint of the forthcoming Devon/Dorset style about it. But it wasn't until October 1951 that the gap was filled with the launch at the Motor Show of a new Seven, the four-door A30, powered by a new 28bhp 803cc overhead-valve engine. Under the RAC rating system the A30 was really an Eight, but with a sharp eye on the market Austin rightly decided to

capitalise on the popularity of its fondly-remembered prewar baby. The Seven was the first Austin to use unitary construction in which the body and floor pan formed a single unit, dispensing with the cost and weight penalties of having a separate chassis.

The A30 was aimed head-on at the market catered for by the popular Morris Minor. The A30 had relatively narrow doors - its wheelbase was only 6ft 7.5in - and a two-door model was added to the range in late 1953, conceived while Austin was still independent but launched after the formation of BMC.

The A30 had independent front suspension and Lockheed hydraulic brakes and weighed only 13cwt against 19cwt for a Devon. This gave it a power-to-weight ratio of 43bhp per ton, broadly comparable with the Devon's figure of 42. It was well-received by buyers, although road testers, gradually moving from the unquestioning acceptance of the 1940s to the outright criticism of later decades did make some adverse comments on engine noise, interior trim and, in *The Autocar* in 1953 on, of all things, the horn, of which the tester wrote: "The horn has a rather weak and impersonal note." But almost 250,000 A30 buyers showed that Austin's new baby was a winner.

The Seven carried some of Austin's styling hallmarks. The grille, topped by the distinctive flying-A symbol, was recognisably related to that on the A70, while moulding lines on the wings echoed the A70's style too.

The original A30 Seven was produced until October 1956 when it was replaced by the improved A35. The A30 was developed as a van and a Countryman estate car, as was the A35 which was also available briefly as a pick-up. The pick-up was short-lived (only 497 were built) because the government decided it was not a commercial vehicle and was therefore liable to purchase tax, which wiped out its price advantage over the saloon.

Work started on a new Seven as early as 1946 when this mock-up was completed of a stylish car with strong overtones of the as yet unseen Devon and Dorset. The rear in particular was pure Devon/Dorset. In the background stands a Sheerline model and another small saloon mock-up with a smoothly profiled rear end.

By 1949, the Seven had metamorphosed into this neat and modern looking two-door coupé with a grille design recognisably that of the A30 and with the flying-A emblem partially ringed by a circle.

When it was launched - to widespread acclaim - the A30 Seven was a compact four door saloon. This publicity photograph taken in November 1951 was intended for use with the background cut out; in it men can be seen working on a Jensen-bodied A40 Sports.

Yet it must be realized that this is a car for economy rather than speed. It is quite lively, and the engine is pleasantly flexible, although it must be admitted that at the top end of the speed range there is a definite impression that parts of the little engine are moving very quickly.
- *from The Autocar road test of an A30, 1952*

A two-door A30 followed in 1953. The photographer clearly wanted a quaint pub and was anxious to get the inn sign in the picture - but for some reason was unhappy about the Midland Red bus company's timetable case, on which he has hung a towel to hide the company's name.

Undoubted highlight of the 1951 Earls Court Show, the new Austin Seven is given a prominence which is at once merited and wise in view of the tremendous public interest in this successor to Lord Austin's original Seven which, appearing shortly after the 1914-18 war, set a world fashion in economy cars and served a wide public throughout almost the whole of the world during the between-wars era.
- *The Motor, 24 October 1951*

The new AUSTIN A30 *Seven*

New assembly building

An artist's impression of the new Car Assembly Building, CAB1, prepared for its official opening.

1951 SAW THE commissioning of the company's new car assembly building, known as CAB1 (Car Assembly Building 1) officially opened in July by the Minister of Supply, George Strauss. Austin produced a brochure to mark the launch which started with a poetic description which few who worked in or visited Longbridge could have immediately recognised:

"The new Austin car assembly building, set amid green lawns and flowerbeds, is the very antithesis of the usually accepted notion of a huge factory. It is constructed in accordance with the most modern ideas of efficiency, yet it has considerable eye-appeal and blends into the surrounding countryside which forms part of one of Birmingham's most popular summer evening and weekend resorts - the Lickey Hills."

The assembly hall had three 250-yard long tracks (with room for a fourth) and was bright and airy, with 60,000sq ft of glass to light it. The

An engine is lowered on to a completed chassis on the CAB1 production line.

Finished and painted bodies were carried on overhead conveyors in a labyrinth of underground tunnels.

A Devon body being mated to its chassis.

tracks were initially used for the A40, A70 and A90, and A135 models. The assembly tracks started in the stores, where there were 750,000 chassis parts. As the frame moved down the track, conveyors were used to supply rear axle and front suspension components, then the engine and finally, after the chassis had passed through electro-static spray booths, the body. These components - including the bodies - reached the assembly hall through a 1,000ft long tunnel.

The result was greater production efficiency. Target output was 2,000 A40s a week, a figure which the new factory came close to achieving in its first 12 months when weekly A40 output actually averaged 1,965. This figure dropped to only 1,625 in 1952/53, but recovered to 2,026 in 1953/54. However in the heady days of 1949-51, weekly A40 output had averaged 2,143.

However even as the new car assembly building was being opened, problems were being experienced in North America, one of Austin's main export markets. In October it was announced that up to 2,500 Austins (and around 2,000 Morrises) were being shipped back from Canada. A tough anti-inflationary Canadian budget was blamed. Some of the cars were re-exported to other left-hand-drive territories while others were converted to right-hand drive for sale in the UK - where a Government-imposed quota of 80,000 new car sales for 1951 was in force as part of a continued postwar austerity programme. Austin's statement said:

"The majority will probably be re-exported but those which will become available to the home market will be converted to right-hand steering and sold in new condition. Such cars will not be sold at a premium price but at the home market price at which they would have been sold if not originally exported to Canada. Those cars will not be extra to the home quota and, therefore, will not in any way affect home deliveries.

"In facing the risk of trading in North America - which on occasion may mean the return of cars to Britain - the Austin Motor Company is adopting a normal manufacturing and sales policy, will itself sustain any loss arising from the double transportation, and will not recover these costs at the expense of the British motoring public."

In Britain the 1951 budget doubled the purchase tax on cars (from 33 to 66 per cent) and in the spring of 1952 the annual home market quota was reduced to 60,000. Buyers of new cars still had to abide by the British Motor Trade Association covenant which controlled the car's resale in an effort to halt profiteering in a market where demand outstripped supply and new car buyers' names were still being added to waiting lists.

A Hereford body is lowered on to its chassis while in the centre of the picture a Devon body is lifted out of the tunnel below.

Two views of the finishing shop showing the exhortation to export at the end of the line. A busy docks scene captioned "The ships are waiting" was backed by a map of the world at a time when large areas of the map were covered in red to mark the extent of the British empire, and when much of the world was genuine Austin sales territory. Both views show A70 Herefords and A40 Devons.

1952: the last real Austin

AUSTIN A40 *Somerset Saloon*

In its new form the A40 is a useful and attractive general purpose car. It provides comfortable travel for four people, has a useful turn of speed for everyday requirements, and under favourable conditions can average 40 m.p.h. The engine is very smooth and silent and there is very little pinking on Pool petrol. Top gear flexibility in traffic conditions is also good. Normal main road gradients of the less steep variety can be climbed on top gear, yet third gear is often kinder, especially if the car is well laden.
- from The Autocar Somerset road test, 1952

THE A40 SOMERSET was, it can be argued, the last real Austin. It was launched in February 1952, when road tax was just £10 a year and the discussions on the merger between Austin and the Nuffield Group were about to bear fruition. A statement outlining the terms of the amalgamation had been issued in November 1951. It was also significant as the last Austin to be launched which featured a separate chassis and body - the chassis was little changed from that of the Devon which it replaced. At its launch the Somerset was listed at £727 18s 11d, which was £15 11s 2d more than the basic Devon.

The A40 Somerset looked like a scaled-down A70 Hereford and in a piece of production planning which would be applauded today even used the same doors as the bigger A70 model. Indeed when the first prototypes for a rebodied Devon were completed, by May 1949, it had already been decided that it would use the doors of the yet-to-be-released Hereford. By August 1950 the Somerset shape had been settled apart from some minor trim details.

Having found no market for the two-door Dorset, Austin only offered the Somerset saloon with four doors. A two-door convertible coupé was made (again, as on the A70, by Carbodies), rectifying an omission from the Devon/Dorset range, and this effectively replaced the A40 Sports. It also sold rather better than the plainly-styled Sports had. A total of 7,243 Somerset coupés was built of which 3,939 were exported, including some which worked as exotic taxis in Bermuda.

The 1200cc engine in the Somerset was rated at 42bhp, compared with 40bhp in the Devon. This modest increase in power was achieved by using the cylinder head from the A40 Sports which had bigger inlet valves and stronger valve springs. The

rear axle ratio on the Somerset was changed to 5.28 from the Devon's 5.14.

The new body offered more interior room (it was 1.5in wider inside) and easier entry by way of its wider doors. The Somerset was 6in longer than the Devon and the central door pillars were 4in further back. The front doors were thus 4in wider than those on the Devon, while the rear doors were a remarkable 8in wider.

The company still had an eye on dollar earnings and exported Somersets to the USA, but the market had changed and the Somerset did not have quite the same success abroad as the Devon had had. However it still proved to be a good seller - over 2 years it notched up 166,000 sales worldwide as a saloon and a further 7,000-plus as a convertible.

As part of its US sales drive Austin encouraged Americans visiting Britain to order a car before leaving home, collecting it on arrival in the UK and then having it shipped back to America when its owners had finished their British holiday. A brochure - "See the old country in a new Austin" - set out the details of Austin's "Britain-and-back" car purchase plan. Buyers could collect their new car from the factory (and have a factory tour), from Austin's London office at 479-483 Oxford Street (telephone Mayfair 7620) or from any one of Austin's 1,000 agents. Directions to the factory from central Birmingham advised would-be buyers that the journey took 40 minutes by tram, 25 minutes by bus or 20 minutes by taxi.

And, in the days before jet crossings of the Atlantic Ocean, Austin said that provided they had four weeks notice the car would be shipped back to the USA on the same vessel as its owners. The cars available under the "Britain-and-back" plan were the A40 Somerset, A40 Sports, A70 Hereford, A90 Atlantic and A125 Sheerline.

One of Britain's attractions for foreign visitors in 1952 and 1953 was the excitement of a new Queen and Austin marked the occasion with a range of special colours with royal connotations - Buckingham Green, Balmoral Blue, Windsor Grey, Sandringham Fawn and Coronet Cream.

For those Britons fortunate enough to be able to holiday abroad, one of Austin's South African distributors, Robbs of Cape Town, offered cars under a guaranteed buy-back scheme for holiday visitors to South Africa.

The new car inspired yet another Alan Hess Austin adventure: to drive from the Equator to the Arctic Circle in a Somerset, a story which Hess chronicled in *Crazy Journey*. Originally Hess had planned to drive from the Arctic Circle in Alaska to Quito in Ecuador, but had to abandon this because of the absence of through roads in Panama and Costa Rica. Instead the trip started in Entebbe in Uganda at 10.03am on 17 March 1953 and then headed up via the Sudan and Egypt with the intention of driving along the North African coast to Tunis, catching a ferry to Marseilles and then driving through Europe to Jokkmokk in Sweden. It almost ended in disaster. They were required to have a police-appointed escort across the Nubian Desert. The escort's vehicle was unreliable and broke down with monotonous regularity, stretching the Austin team's resources. A planned 13 hour journey took three days and Hess and his two colleagues, Ken Wharton and Ronald Jeavons, ran out of water. They were rescued by a railway repair team as the vultures wheeled overhead waiting for them to die.

Because they were running late, instead of driving to Tunis they had the car flown from Cairo to Marseilles in a chartered KLM Skymaster plane and actually reached the Arctic Circle at 6.05pm on 28 March, 11 days after leaving the Equator. They covered 7,673 miles.

After years of pool petrol, premium grades were once again made available in 1953 and from 1 February for an extra 2d, 3d or 4d a gallon motorists could buy higher grades of fuel. The standard petrol price had climbed to around 4s 3d a gallon. The use of premium grade fuels suited the modern A40 engine admirably, improving its performance and eliminating pinking.

The Somerset body was not offered as a van or a chassis/scuttle and A40 commercials continued to use the Devon-derived front end, but with the 42bhp Somerset engine and chassis. A Somerset-based van prototype was built but never reached production.

Suddenly and without warning we plunged from reasonably firm going into deep sand. A quick change down to third and our revs were still dying on us, another quick change to second and then to bottom and we just struggled through, but this was only the beginning - a few minutes later the same thing happened again, but this time the sand was deeper and more extensive and even in bottom gear we couldn't get clear of it.

Out came the sand-tracks and shovels and with the help of the two natives from the Pickup we were soon on the move once more; however, from this point on both our own car and the escort were repeatedly brought to a halt.

- Alan Hess, writing in Crazy Journey.

Leonard Lord took a personal interest in styling. Photographs of the mock-up illustrated right are pinned to his drawing board.

This mock-up was photographed at the same time as the car above and shows something much closer to the design which Austin pursued. The front wing line is that which was adopted for the new A40 and the roof line is about right too. It stands on a solid steel table, built to provide an absolutely flat surface to ensure accuracy in the dimensions of the mock-ups.

One attempt to create a replacement for the A40 Devon which was taking shape in January 1949 looked like a toned-down Atlantic. It was in many ways a more advanced design than that which was actually chosen. Smooth-sided bodies were the shape of the future. Tantalising bits in the background include what appear to be a full-size mock up of a Sheerline front end, a K-series truck bonnet and, on the right, a forward-control truck cab.

By May 1949 the design had evolved and this prototype was available for inspection. It uses the doors of the A70 Hereford (which was not to be revealed for another 18 months), but with a simpler grille surmounted by a winged motif and a flying-A which is partly enclosed by a circle. A separate side light is provided on the driver's side of the car only; the passenger's side presumably had an integrated head and side light as used on early Devons.

Austin's postwar export markets included Japan, where there were over 1,000 Austins in use. The company's reputation was such that Nissan, seeking to update its products and its production methods, turned to Austin for help. The result was the signing in December 1952 of a historic agreement whereby Nissan would assemble Somerset kits in Japan, with a target production rate of 2,000 a year. The first Nissan-built Somerset was completed in April 1953. The agreement included a clause whereby the local content of the cars would be increased. It reached 50 per cent at the end of 1954, shortly before Nissan ceased building Somersets and started building the new Cambridge.

For use by disabled drivers Austin offered a Somerset with hand controls. A quadrant-shaped lever below the rim of the steering wheel operated the brakes. A trigger attached to the gear lever was used to actuate the clutch. A hand-operated accelerator was mounted on the steering column. To assist with the operation of the clutch and brakes Austin fitted a vacuum servo. Vehicles equipped with hand controls retained the normal pedals so that other drivers could easily use the car.

In 1946, after 40 years of production, Austin had produced its 1,000,000th car. Only seven years later, towards the end of 1953, it produced its 2,000,000th, a Somerset. During those seven years the company claimed to have exported almost 400,000 A40s and to have earned £230 million - a staggering sum at the time - in foreign currency. The company was one of Britain's leading exporters and a major employer with 19,000 people working on its 160 acre Longbridge site.

Total A40 car production - Devon, Dorset, Somerset and Sports excluding commercial and Countryman derivatives - was a creditable 467,214 which handsomely exceeded the 322,224 of the popular prewar Seven, even if the A40 never did raise quite the same sentimental attachment as the prewar car.

In 1954, the last year of Counties car production, Austin was still selling Somersets in the USA. The A40 sedan, as it was called, would "cut operating costs by 50 per cent" and sold for $1,695, equivalent to the cheapest Chevrolet and Ford models. The A30, a car which must surely have been quite inappropriate for such a big car culture, sold at $1,395.

But exports were a declining proportion of the company's increasing output. In March 1954, when monthly production reached a new record of 20,634, a total of 13,000 vehicles were exported, which was also a monthly record. It still represented over 50 per cent of the company's output, but was well short of the 70-plus per cent of only a few years earlier. The key markets listed in 1954 were:

Australia	2,500
Canada	2,200
USA	2,000
Sweden	1,350
South Africa	600
New Zealand	550

Production of the Somerset ceased in October 1954 (when its road tax had risen to £12 10s) and with it came the end of Austin's line of Counties cars. The Somerset's replacement revived the prewar Cambridge name. Some of the last Somersets to be produced had a bench front seat and a speedometer which featured a small clock, similar to that used in the A70 Hereford.

The new A40 design was pretty well complete by August 1950 when this car, described as a Devon prototype, was photographed. The main changes which would be made before the launch - still 18 months away - were new grilles to flank the main radiator grille, neater sidelights, and the removal of the three slats on the bonnet side where the Austin of England badge would be carried.

A prototype Somerset on test in East Africa with non-standard grilles and bonnet louvres.

The Somerset press launch at London's Grosvenor House on 1 February 1952. Austin's managing director, Leonard Lord, is on the extreme right. The two-tone paint scheme was not a production option.

Some early Somersets lacked the stainless steel trim along the bottom of the doors, as shown on this car photographed in March 1952, just weeks after the launch.

Somerset bodies on the welding lines in the Car Assembly Building, March 1952.

After the roto dip the completed bodies passed through an automated paint plant. Nearest the camera are Somersets, including one tilted over while its roof is given attention. An A40 Countryman is on the conveyor in the background.

Overhead conveyors delivered finished bodies to the chassis track.

Carbodies produced the stylish Somerset coupé which could be driven with the top folded back to the coupé de ville position or fully retracted.

A few coupés found their way to Bermuda for use as taxis.

The Somerset coupé in the USA, complete with whitewall tyres.

Prices: Austin and the competition, July 1952			
	£	s	d
Ford Anglia 8hp	489	3	4
A30 Seven	553	14	5
Morris Minor(4-door)	631	10	0
Triumph Mayflower	701	10	0
A40 Somerset	727	18	11
Hillman Minx	732	12	3
Ford Consul	752	1	1
Vauxhall Wyvern	771	10	0
Morris Oxford	794	16	8
Daimler 3-litre Regency	2334	16	8
Humber Imperial	2490	7	9
A135 Princess	2750	3	4
Bentley Standard Steel	4823	14	5

In Japan, Nissan looked to Austin for help in updating its models and its factories. Somersets were built under licence in Japan. A body is lowered gently on to the chassis (*left*). The first completed Somerset comes off the Nissan assembly line (*below, left*).

The end of the line for Counties Austins. A group of workers raise a cheer for the photographer as the last Somerset comes off the production line on 4 October 1954.

Austin's most ambitious publicity stunt was to drive a Somerset from the Equator to the Arctic Circle in March 1953. The car stands in Uganda with its front wheels in the northern hemisphere and its rear wheels in the southern hemisphere on 17 March. Note the map on the door.

Top, right: The desert crossing taxed both men and machine. The gruelling conditions of the Sahara almost cost the team their lives.

Right: Eleven days after leaving tropical Africa the car was running in sub-zero temperatures in Sweden.

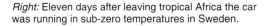

The end of an era

THE SOMERSET MARKED the end of an era. It was the last car totally developed by an independent Austin. During the 2.5 years of Somerset production Austin did build one more car which had strong pre-BMC connections, the Metropolitan. This had been designed by American manufacturer Nash and was unveiled in prototype form in 1950 as the NXI project (Nash Experimental International) and was a scaled-down American car. It was announced in October 1952 that Austin had won the contract to supply the NXI - other contenders to build it had included Standard and Fiat. The success of the A40 in America and the existence of a dealer network to support the 1200cc engine must have been an influence in Nash's choice of Austin as the builder. The NXI appeared as the Metropolitan, a two-door

Austin co-operated with the American Kelvinator Corporation to produce the Metropolitan, a scaled-down Nash powered by the A40's 1200cc engine. It was initially sold only in North America.

convertible or hardtop coupé with bodywork by Fisher & Ludlow which used the Somerset's 42bhp 1200cc engine coupled to a modified version of the A40's gearbox with only three speeds. It used the A30's independent front suspension and live rear axle. Production started in the autumn of 1953 for the American launch in the spring of 1954. The Metropolitan was shown to the British press in March 1954 by which time 3,000 cars had already been shipped to the USA and Canada. The Metropolitan was a colourful little car and at the press launch George Harriman, Austin's deputy chairman, said with disarming frankness: "Did we choose the colours? No, we paint them to Nash requirements. Even if you don't like them, you can be sure the Americans do."

The Motor's road testers were also struck by the colour: "Unusual in appearance, and conspicuous in a pink-and-cream colour scheme, the Nash Metropolitan submitted for test was too flamboyant looking to please everyone, but a substantial proportion of those who saw it in town and country surroundings were favourably impressed." Over at *The Autocar* the road tester concluded somewhat ambiguously: "The Nash Metropolitan is a unique example of Anglo-American co-operation and should be well suited for the work it is intended to do."

Harriman said at the Metropolitan launch that Austin had exported over $120 million worth of cars to the USA and that in the week before the launch the company had shipped 887 cars worth nearly $1 million. The Metropolitan continued in its original form until the end of 1955 when an uprated 1.5-litre model was launched. This was made available to British buyers from the spring of 1957.

BMC

AUSTIN AND THE Nuffield group were merged in 1952. The new organisation, the British Motor Corporation, employed 42,000 people and produced 300,000 cars a year which made it the biggest car builder outside the USA and number four in the world after Ford, General Motors and Chrysler.

There had been earlier talks which had come to nought, but now the die was cast. Leonard Lord, ex-Morris and now head of Austin, took control of the new British Motor Corporation. Austin was the dominant partner in the new combine which was now market leader in Britain. New models were developed with ADO - Austin Drawing Office - numbers.

There were no speedy moves towards rationalisation. The Austin and Nuffield dealer networks and the models they sold continued largely unchanged - apart from the installation of the Austin A30's overhead valve engine in the Morris Minor. By the end of the decade rationalisation, and badge engineering as it became known, started. BMC's mid-range saloons from Austin, Morris, MG, Riley and Wolseley all shared the same Farina-designed body shell.

The story of the following three decades is a sad one of decline. Suffice it to say here that the Austin name survived until 1988 when the last cars to carry it, the Maestro and Montego, were promoted as brands in their own right by the Rover Group.

New-look A125

THE DOORS WHICH the A40 Somerset shared with the A70 Hereford almost found use on one more model - a new-look A125. A prototype was assembled in June 1951 which used the sweeping Hereford door/ wing line on an A125 chassis. The rear end looked like an extended A30 and the whole ensemble was, to say the least, a trifle ungainly. However 12 months later a much improved version appeared, complete with Atlantic-style three-piece wraparound rear window. But with A125/A135 sales volumes having plummeted to around one-tenth of what they had been, there was no place for this stylish update.

The doors which served on both the A70 Hereford and A40 Somerset were used in an aborted attempt to restyle the A125 models. The summer 1951 prototype was a strange blend of styles. From the front it had some of the presence of the big Jaguar cars, but the rear was an unhappy amalgam of Atlantic-style three-piece wraparound window and a heavy-looking boot which resembled that used on the 1954 Cambridge. The spare wheel was housed in a separate compartment below the boot.

Twelve months later a slightly more stylish prototype appeared. The radiator grille was less distinctive but the flowing wing line was neater and the rear end, although still with three-piece window, was much tidier and looked less heavy.

The end

WHEN THE SOMERSET was replaced in 1954, its successor appeared as the A40 and A50 Cambridge. This was another monocoque car, following the example set by the A30, and it used the BMC B-series 1200cc engine, which was also fitted to the competing Morris Cowley launched in the same year. Although the new A40's engine was of the same capacity as the Somerset's, it was not the same engine; the BMC B-series was slightly larger than the Austin engine.

The new Cambridge had a body style unique to Austin. The next generation of Cambridges, launched in 1959, had Farina-styled body shells which they shared with BMC's other marques - Morris, Riley, MG and Wolseley.

Even as the Somerset was being launched, Austin's designers were planning its replacement. These models were completed in March 1952 and show a blend of the design features of the Somerset and its successor, the Cambridge.

By May, the models were much closer to the final Cambridge design.

The A40 Cambridge was initially produced in two- and four-door variants. This is a rare two-door car, photographed in November 1954.

The End. A March 1953 view of a Somerset carrying a BMC rosette with the Austin name on it - one piece of badge engineering which did not come to pass.

Somersets on the lower deck and Herefords on the top deck of a Carrimore trailer pulled by a K-series tractor operated by Austin's Plymouth distributor, A C Turner.

Table 1
Austin models, 1939-54

This table summarises the cars and car-derived light commercial vehicles produced by Austin between 1939 and 1954. The introduction dates given are generally launch dates; production dates are liable to be different.

Name	Model code	Introduced	Discontinued
PREWAR			
Eight 4-door	AR	February 1939	1942
Eight 2-door	ARA	February 1939	1942
Eight tourer	AP	February 1939	1942
Eight van	AV	February 1939	1940
Ten saloon	GRQ	May 1939	1945
Ten tourer	GQC	May 1939	1940
Ten van	GVE	May 1939	1940
Twelve	HRB	August 1939	1940
POSTWAR			
The first postwar model range			
Eight 4-door	AS1	August 1945	October 1947
Eight van	AV1	August 1945	October 1947
Ten	GS1	August 1945	October 1947
Ten van	GV1	August 1945	October 1947
Twelve	HS1	August 1945	October 1947
Sixteen	BS1	August 1945	March 1949
Sixteen Countryman	BW1	May 1947	October 1949
The A40 range			
A40 Devon	GS2	October 1947	August 1951
A40 Devon MkII	GS2A	May 1949	August 1951
A40 Devon	GS3	August 1951	February 1952
A40 Dorset	G2S2	October 1947	October 1949
A40 10cwt van	GV2	March 1948	May 1951
A40 10cwt van	GV3	May 1951	August 1951
A40 10cwt van	GV4	August 1951	August 1954
A40 10cwt van	GV5	September 1954	March 1957
A40 pick-up	GQU2	September 1948	May 1951
A40 pick-up	GQU3	May 1951	August 1951
A40 pick-up	GQU4	August 1951	August 1954
A40 pick-up	GQU5	September 1954	March 1957
A40 Countryman	GP2	September 1948	May 1951
A40 Countryman	GP3	May 1951	August 1951
A40 Countryman	GP4	August 1951	August 1954
A40 Countryman	GP5	September 1954	March 1957
A40 chassis/cab	GQ4	September 1951	August 1954
A40 chassis/cab	GQ5	September 1954	March 1957
A40 chassis/scuttle	GVR5	September 1954	March 1957
A40 Sports	GD2	October 1950	August 1951
A40 Sports	GD3	August 1951	June 1953
A40 Somerset	GS4	February 1952	October 1954
A40 Somerset coupe	GD5	March 1952	October 1954
The A70 range			
A70 Hampshire	BS2	September 1948	October 1950
A70 pick-up	BQU2	September 1949	March 1951
A70 Countryman	BW3	January 1950	March 1951
A70 Hereford	BS3	October 1950	October 1954
A70 Hereford coupe	BD3	November 1951	August 1952
A70 pick-up	BK3	June 1951	October 1954
A70 chassis/cab	BQ3	June 1951	October 1954
A70 chassis/scuttle	BQR3	June 1951	October 1954
A70 Countryman	BW4	June 1951	October 1954
The A90 range			
A90 Atlantic coupé	BD2	September 1948	November 1950
A90 Atlantic saloon	BE2	September 1949	December 1952
The Sheerline range			
A125 Sheerline swb	DS1	February 1947	August 1954
A125 Sheerline lwb	DM1	October 1949	October 1953
A125 ambulance	DA1	February 1947	October 1955
A125 hearse	DH1	February 1947	October 1955
The Vanden Plas Princess range			
A135 Princess	DS2	February 1948	October 1950
A135 Princess II	DS3	October 1950	October 1953
A135 Princess III	DS5	October 1953	July 1956

Model	Code	From	To	Model	Code	From	To
A135 limousine	DM2	October 1948	September 1950	A30 Seven 2-door	A2S4	October 1953	October 1956
A135 II limousine	DM3	October 1950	April 1953	A30 Countryman	AP4	October 1954	October 1956
A135 III limousine	DM5	May 1953	February 1956	A30 Van	AV4	October 1954	October 1956
A135 limousine lwb	DM4	October 1952	March 1968	**Other models**			
A135 Princess lwb	DS6	October 1953	March 1968				
				Hire car	FL1	March 1949	1958
The A30 range				Taxi	FX3	June 1948	1958
				Austin-Healey	BN1	May 1953	September 1955
A30 Seven 4-door	AS3	October 1951	October 1953	Metropolitan	NK1	August 1953	December 1955
A30 Seven 4-door	AS4	October 1953	October 1956				

Table 2

Austin: the postwar model codes

An alphabetical listing of all Austin-style model codes used for postwar cars and car-related models, including those developed by BMC. As a general rule the first letter indicates the engine size and the second letter the body style.

Code	Model	Code	Model	Code	Model
AK5	A35 pick-up	BS5	A105 Westminster	G2T2	A40 tourer (Australia)
AP4	A30 Countryman	BS6	A95 Westminster	GP3	A40 Countryman
AP5	A35 Countryman	BS7	A105 Westminster	GP4	A40 Countryman
AP6	A35 MkII Countryman	BS8	A105 Westminster Vanden Plas	GP5	A40 Countryman
AS1	Eight 4-door	BS9	A99 Farina	GQ4	A40 chassis/cab
AS3	A30 4-door	BS10	A110 Farina	GQ5	A40 chassis/cab
AS4	A30 4-door	BS11	A110 MkII Farina	GQU2	A40 pick-up
A2S4	A30 2-door			GQU3	A40 pick-up
		BT7	Austin-Healey 3000 2+2	GQU4	A40 pick-up
AS5	A35 4-door			GQU5	A40 pick-up
A2S5	A35 2-door	BW1	Sixteen Countryman		
A2S6	A40 Farina saloon	BW3	A70 Hampshire Countryman	GS1	Ten 4-door
A2S8	A40 Farina MkII	BW4	A70 Hereford Countryman	GS2	A40 Devon
A2S9	A40 Farina MkII	BW6	A95 Westminster Countryman	GS2A	A40 Devon MkII
AS10	1100 4-door saloon			GS2B	A40 Devon (for Bermuda)
A2S10	1100 2-door saloon	DA1	A125 ambulance	G2S2	A40 Dorset
A2W10	1100 Countryman	DA2	A135 ambulance	G2S2B	A40 Dorset (for Bermuda)
		DH1	A125 hearse	GS3	A40 Devon
AV1	Eight van	DH2	A135 hearse	GS4	A40 Somerset
AV4	A30 5cwt van	DM1	A125 Sheerline limousine lwb	GS5	A40 Cambridge 4-door
AV5	A35 5cwt van	DM2	A135 Princess touring limousine	G2S5	A40 Cambridge 2-door
AV6	A35 MkII 5cwt van	DM3	A135 Princess touring limousine MkII		
AV8	A35 MkIII 6cwt van			GV1	Ten van
		DM4	A135 Princess lwb limousine MkIII	GV2	A40 10cwt van
AW6	A40 Farina Countryman	DM5	A135 Princess swb limousine MkIII	GV2B	A40 10cwt van (for Bermuda)
AW8	A40 Farina Countryman	DM7	A135 Princess touring limousine MkIV	GV3	A40 10cwt van
AW9	A40 Farina MkII Countryman			GV4	A40 10cwt van
		DS1	A125 Sheerline swb	GV5	A40 10cwt van
BD2	A90 Atlantic coupé	DS2	A135 Princess swb	GVR5	A40 chassis/scuttle
BD3	A70 Hereford coupé	DS3	A135 Princess swb MkII		
		DS5	A135 Princess swb MkIII	HD6	Metropolitan 1500 convertible
BE2	A90 Atlantic hardtop	DS6	A135 Princess lwb MkIII	HE6	Metropolitan 1500 hardtop
		DS7	A135 Princess MkIV	HJ7	Metropolitan 1500 convertible
BK3	A70 Hereford pick-up			HK6	A50 Cambridge pick-up
		FL1	Hire car	HP7	Metropolitan 1500 hardtop
BN1	Austin-Healey 100	FL1D	Hire car, diesel		
BN2	Austin-Healey 100	FL2D	Hire car, diesel	HS1	Twelve
BN4	Austin-Healey 100-Six	FX3	Taxi	HS5	A50 Cambridge
BN6	Austin-Healey 100-Six	FX3D	Taxi, diesel	HS6	A55 Cambridge
BN7	Austin-Healey 3000	FX4	Taxi	HS8	A55 Cambridge MkII Farina
		FX4D	Taxi, diesel	HS10	1800 saloon
BQ3	A70 Hereford chassis/cab				
BQR3	A70 Hereford chassis/scuttle	GD2	A40 Sports	HV6	A50 Cambridge 1/2-ton van
BQU2	A70 Hampshire pick-up	GD3	A40 Sports	HW9	A55 Cambridge Countryman
		GD5	A40 Somerset coupé		
BS1	Sixteen			NK1	Nash Metropolitan
BS2	A70 Hampshire	GP2	A40 Countryman		
BS3	A70 Hereford	GP2B	A40 Countryman (for Bermuda)		
BS4	A90 Westminster Six				

Left hand drive models were generally denoted by an L suffix.

Table 3

Annual production, 8, 10, 12 and 16

Model	Total volume	1938/39	1939/40	1940/41	1941/42	1942/43	1943/44	1944/45	1945/46	1946/47	1947/48	1948/49
Eight	103,585	17447	24230	5064	707	34	0	0	15169	31619	9315	
Ten	106,809*	7000*	11290	11645	3749	5922	6886	4796	19508	28247	7766	
Twelve	10,628		1924	6	0	0	0	0	1816	5914	968	
Sixteen	35,434								2270	7003	15157	11004

* estimated

Table 4
Annual production, Counties models

Model	Total volume	1947/48	1948/49	1949/50	1950/51	1951/52	1952/53	1953/54	1954/55	1955/56	1956/57
A40 Devon	273,958	22817	61275	81046	79383	29437					
A40 Dorset	15,939	8033	7736	170							
A40 Sports	4,011				552	2610	849				
A40 Somerset	166,063					38131	54812	71117	2003		
A40 Somerset coupe	7,243					28	4296	2908	11		
A40 Countryman	26,587		2007	4792	6104	3221	3061	2933	2914	1466	89
A40 van	78,242	1920	7945	7774	6144	7520	9052	14650	11454	11369	414
A40 pick-up	61,818		4787	8267	11580	13351	5959	5675	6959	4698	542
A40 TOTAL	633,861	32770	83750	102049	103763	94298	78029	97283	23341	17533	1045
A70 Hampshire	34,360		5636	19833	8891						
A70 Hampshire Countryman	901			336	565						
A70 Hereford	48,640				4927	15585	15912	10446	1770		
A70 Hereford Countryman	1,515				34	680	470	301	30		
A70 Hereford coupe	266					236	30				
A70 pick-up	20,434			2805	7245	6966	1832	1459	127		
A70 TOTAL	106,116		5636	22974	21662	23467	18244	12206	1927		
A90 Atlantic	7,981		405	2694	2553	2093	236				

Table 5
Total production volumes, other models

A125/A135 (1947-68)	15,120	Metropolitan (1953-60)	104,377
A30 (1951-56)	222,837	K8 25cwt van (1947-54)	27,042
A35 (1956-68)	353,835	Taxi/hire car (1947-60)	15,453

Table 6
1950 Austin prices

Cars

A40 Devon MkI saloon, fixed head	£501	12s	10d
A40 Devon MkI saloon, sliding head	£505	9s	5d
A40 Devon MkII saloon, fixed head	£447	19s	5d
A40 Countryman, passenger van	£569	7s	3d
A70 Hampshire saloon, fixed head	£648	11s	8d
A70 Hampshire saloon, sliding head	£658	16s	1d
A70 Countryman	£761	0s	7d
A90 Atlantic convertible (standard)	£914	7s	3d
A90 Atlantic convertible (power operated hood)	£952	13s	11d
A90 Atlantic Sports saloon	£1016	11s	8d
FL1 hire car	£971	17s	3d
A125 Sheerline saloon	£1597	19s	5d
A125 Sheerline limousine	£1783	5s	0d
A125 Sheerline ambulance	£1525	0s	0d
A135 Princess sports saloon	£1821	11s	8d
A135 Princess touring limousine	£1981	6s	1d
Toy car - Pathfinder special	£16	7s	0d
Toy car - J40 roadster	£20	9s	4d

Optional extras

A40 heater	£7	13s	4d
A40 radio	£31	18s	10d
A70 radio	£40	5s	0d
A90 radio	£40	5s	0d

Vans

A40 10cwt van	in colour	£432	8s	4d
	in grey priming	£422	8s	4d
A40 10cwt pick-up	in colour	£432	8s	4d
	in grey priming	£422	8s	4d
A70 15cwt pick-up	in colour	£556	0s	7d
	in grey priming	£546	0s	7d
25cwt chassis		£560	8s	4d
	chassis and open-backed cab in grey priming	£617	8s	4d
	chassis and enclosed cab in grey priming	£627	8s	4d
	'Three-way' van in grey priming	£767	8s	4d

Loadstar trucks in grey priming

2-ton lwb chassis		£561	13s	11d
	chassis and cab	£630	13s	11d
	platform truck	£682	13s	11d
	dropside truck	£687	13s	11d
5-ton lwb chassis		£680	10s	7d
	chassis and cab	£748	10s	7d
	platform truck	£816	10s	7d
	dropside truck	£826	10s	7d
5-ton swb chassis		£663	18s	4d
	chassis and cab	£729	18s	4d
	hydraulic tipper	£844	18s	4d
Coach - chassis only		£741	17s	3d

Additional equipment

controlled ventilation, cab insulation and sliding rear window	£12	0s	0d
single heater/demister	£7	0s	0d
dual heater/demister	£12	10s	0d
hinged window quarter lights	£1	0s	0d

A standard Somerset, posed in Broadway in the Cotswolds in the autumn of 1952.

Table 7
Selected specifications

Model	Code	cc	bhp	Wheelbase		Length		Width		Weight	Tyres
				ft	in	ft	in	ft	in	cwt	
Eight	AS1	900	24	7	4.50	12	5	4	8	15.25	4.50-17
Ten	GS1	1125	32	7	9.75	13	2	4	10.50	17.75	5.00-16
Twelve	HS1	1535	40	8	8.50	14	3	5	7	24.25	5.50-16
Sixteen	BS1	2199	67	8	8.50	14	3	5	7	26.50	5.75-16
A40 Devon	GS2	1200	40	7	8.50	12	9.25	5	1	19	5.25-16
A40 Sports	GD2	1200	46	7	8.50	13	3.25	5	1.25	19	5.25-16
A40 Somerset	GS4	1200	42	7	8.50	13	3.50	5	3	19.25	5.25-16
A40 van	GV4	1200	42	7	8.50	13	3.50	5	4.50	18.25	5.00-17
A70 Hampshire	BS2	2199	67	8	0	13	7.25	5	6	25	5.50-16
A70 Hereford	BS3	2199	67	8	3	13	10.50	5	9.50	24.50	5.50-16
A70 pick-up	BK3	2199	67	8	7.50	14	1.25	5	10	24	6.00-17
A90 Atlantic	BD2	2660	88	8	0	14	9.25	5	10	26.25	5.50-16
Taxi	FX3	2199	52	9	2.50	14	5.25	5	7.50	28.25	5.75-16
A30 Seven	AS2	803	28	6	7.50	11	4.50	4	7.25	13.50	5.20-13
A125 Sheerline	DS1	3993	125	9	11.25	16	0	6	1	37	6.50-16
A135 Princess	DS2	3993	130	9	11.25	16	0.50	6	0.50	38	6.50-16
A135 Princess	DM4	3993	125	11	0	17	11	6	2.50	41.75	6.50-16

Table 8
The postwar car launches

1945	Sixteen
1947	A40 Devon
	A40 Dorset
	A125 Sheerline
1948	A70 Hampshire
	A90 Atlantic
	A135 Princess
1950	A40 Sports
	A70 Hereford
1951	A30 Seven
1952	A40 Somerset
1953	Austin-Healey
	Metropolitan

Table 9
Pedal Car Model Codes

JOY 1	1946	Austin 8/10 based prototype
JOY 2	1947	A40 based prototype
JOY 3	1949	production Pathfinder Special
JOY 4 (J40)	late 1949	production Devon style roadster